wtf1.

ANNUAL

2022

WTF1 Annual 2022

Written by Katy Fairman

Cover / Art Direction Oliver Card

Editorial Director   Andrew Van de Burgt
Sub-editor   Ben Anderson
Graphics   Oliver Card / Paul Carpenter
Additional Content   Tom Bellingham / Matt Gallagher

Printer   Gomer Press Ltd in Wales, UK
Distribution   CBL Distribution Ltd.
Publisher   The Race Media Ltd.

CONTENTS

Foreword by The Founder 4
The Cars: Big Changes for 2022 6
F101 What is Porpoising? 8
ROUND 01 Bahrain 10
All Aboard The Hype Train 13
ROUND 02 Saudi Arabia 14
Tommy's Helmet Design Challenge 17
ROUND 03 Australia 18
F101 A Guide to Tyres in F1 22
ROUND 04 Emilia Romagna 24
Connect The Dots with Guenther Steiner 27
ROUND 05 Miami 28
Matt's Miami GP Diary 31
Can Katy Survive Karting? 32
ROUND 06 Spain 34
All about the 2022 Aston Martin F1 Safety Car 37
ROUND 07 Monaco 38
ROUND 08 Azerbaijan 42
WTF1-to-1 with Sebastian Vettel 45
ROUND 09 Canada 46
Guess the Circuit 49
ROUND 10 Great Britain 50
Team WTF1 Fan Cam at Silverstone 54
WTF1 Clubhouse 2022 56
ROUND 11 Austria 58
F101 Why Don't F1 Cars Have Handbrakes? 61

ROUND 12 France
Team Principal Anagram Challenge
ROUND 13 Hungary
WTF1-to-1 with Jenson Button
Piastrigate: WTF1 Crack the Case
ROUND 14 Belgium
Dear Katy...
ROUND 15 Netherlands
Ferrari's Wheel of Misfortune
ROUND 16 Italy
Tommy's Livery Challenge
ROUND 17 Singapore
F101 Stay Cool Baby
ROUND 18 Japan
ROUND 19 United States
Hot Takes Wednesday
Team WTF1 Global Fan Gallery
ROUND 20 Mexico City
Seb's Legacy
ROUND 21 São Paulo
ROUND 22 Abu Dhabi
Final Standings
ABCDEF1
Final Thoughts
Answers
Acknowledgements

The WTF1 Annual is back! It's been great to follow the 2022 season, which began a brand new era of F1.

While we didn't see the same titanic championship battle as in 2021, the new regulations did provide us with a shake-up and much closer racing on track - and boy has there been some drama!

Who would have thought when the **Ferrari Hype Train** was in full flow in Bahrain (and Matt at maximum smugness) we'd see Max Verstappen not only overturn the biggest deficit in championship history but win it with a record number of race victories and points haul.

That leads me onto the first off-track memory this year and the introduction of **WTF1 on Twitch**, where this amazing community watched the races with us live, witnessing our uncut reactions to every dramatic moment and Ferrari fumble.

Speaking of Ferrari, Matt headed over to **Miami** early on in the season and finally got to film a video with the love of his life, **Charles Leclerc**, and then again at the season finale in Abu Dhabi.

In another first, 'The Author' Katy got behind the wheel of a kart this year. She was coached by W Series legend **Alice Powell**, with impressive results.

And how could we forget the second addition of the **WTF1 Clubhouse**, which was bigger and better than ever, as we partied with our amazing **Team WTF1** members, recorded live videos and podcasts, as well as sitting back and enjoying the Fake Marina!

Speaking of podcasts, we were even lucky enough to win a **Sports Podcast Award** this year, meaning our F1 ramblings are now prize-winning! A big thank you to everyone who voted to make that possible.

Finally from myself, Matt, Katy, and everyone else behind the scenes, thank you for continuously supporting us every step of the way and sharing our love for Formula 1. We hope you enjoy reading this annual as much as we did writing it.

Be sure to share your pictures with your copy of the WTF1 Annual with **@wtf1official** using the hashtag **#wtf1annual** on social media!

Thank you again, and enjoy the book!

Lots of love,

Tommy

FOREWORD

THE PRESENTER
MATT
@MATTYWTF1

THE FOUNDER
TOMMY
@TOMMYWTF1

THE AUTHOR
KATY
@KATYFAIRMAN

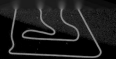
BAHRAIN
GRAND PRIX
18 - 20 MAR

SAUDI ARABIAN
GRAND PRIX
25 - 27 MAR

AUSTRALIAN
GRAND PRIX
08 - 10 APR

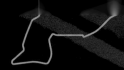
EMILIA ROMAGNA
GRAND PRIX
22 - 24 APR

MIAMI
GRAND PRIX
06 - 08 MAY

SPANISH
GRAND PRIX
20 - 22 MAY

MONACO
GRAND PRIX
27 - 29 MAY

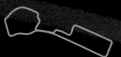
AZERBAIJAN
GRAND PRIX
10 - 12 JUN

CANADIAN
GRAND PRIX
17 - 19 JUN

BRITISH
GRAND PRIX
01 - 03 JUL

AUSTRIAN
GRAND PRIX
08 - 10 JUL

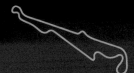
FRENCH
GRAND PRIX
22 - 24 JUL

HUNGARIAN
GRAND PRIX
29 - 31 JUL

BELGIAN
GRAND PRIX
26 - 28 AUG

NETHERLANDS
GRAND PRIX
02 - 04 SEP

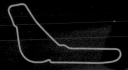
ITALIAN
GRAND PRIX
09 - 11 SEP

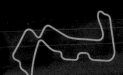
SINGAPORE
GRAND PRIX
30 SEP - 02 OCT

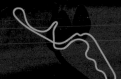
JAPANESE
GRAND PRIX
07 - 09 OCT

UNITED STATES
GRAND PRIX
21 - 23 OCT

MEXICAN
GRAND PRIX
28 - 30 OCT

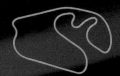
BRAZILIAN
GRAND PRIX
11 - 13 NOV

ABU DHABI
GRAND PRIX
18 - 20 NOV

2022 SEASON CALENDAR

FLOOR

Ground effect makes a return, having first been seen in F1 back in the mid-to-late 1970s. The idea is to create downforce by using the floor to suck the car towards the circuit from underneath, relying less on the wings and upper surfaces to push the car down, which creates turbulence. The 2022 cars also feature underfloor tunnels for air to pass through.

FRONT WING

This part of the car has been massively simplified. The shape has dramatically changed, with four wing elements and a very different-looking endplate. By having the design more stripped back, it should benefit the following cars to be less sensitive to the leading car which now directs airflow in a less disruptive manner.

MMM, LOVE THAT
NEW CAR SMELL

THE CARS:
BIG CHANGES
FOR 2022

FUEL

Inside the cars, the fuel for the power units has undergone a small but significant change. The new E10 blend, which now contains 10% ethanol - up from 5% previously - means lower CO_2 emissions. This new fuel mixture also affects the performance of the car and has required the engine manufacturers to alter their combustion processes.

REAR WING

The Drag Reduction System (DRS) is still a key part of the 2022 rear wing. It's another minimalistic design, with the straight endplates we're used to seeing being much more curved. The rear wing design helps the airflow from the leading car go up and over the following car, which should make it easier to follow.

WHEELS & TYRES

F1 is using 18-inch wheels from the 2022 season, an increase from the previous 13-inch design. They'll overheat less and can be pushed harder for longer which should encourage more overtaking. There are also mandatory wheel covers for the first time since 2009, and 'winglets' which sit over the wheels and push air around the rear wing.

WEIGHT

Modern F1 cars just continue to get heavier! Wheels and tyres are now larger, and weigh 14kg more than they did last season. Extra safety precautions to pass crash tests also means the total weight of the cars has increased by 5%, from 752kg to around 790kg. Several teams also struggled with the weight limit at the start of the season, with many being over what the rules stated!

F1O1

Answering all your questions about Formula 1

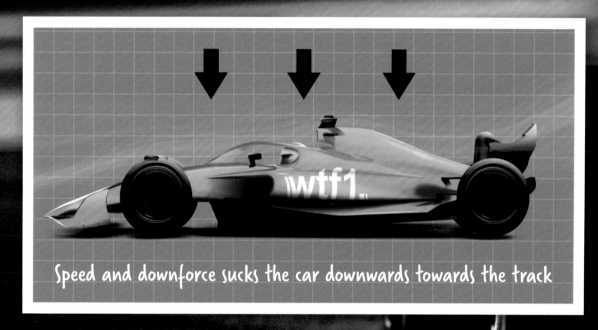

Speed and downforce sucks the car downwards towards the track

WHAT IS PORPOISING?

With a new generation of cars, there's bound to be some teething issues. However, there was one BIG problem for teams up and down the grid which was apparent after the first day of pre-season testing: bouncing. LOTS of bouncing.

As drivers took to their new cars, and found themselves bobbing up and down and excessively jiggling around in their cockpits, it was clear that this probably wasn't part of the plan.

Soon, the term 'porpoising' became a big part of every F1 fan's vocabulary, but what is it?

The aerodynamic phenomenon of porpoising is nothing new, and is commonly seen on cars using ground effect aerodynamics. This is due to the speed and downforce which sucks the car down towards the track.

As the car gets faster, the ride height - which is the height between the bottom of the car and the track's surface - decreases.

This can disrupt the airflow underneath the car, reduce downforce suddenly, which then results in a bouncing effect, known as porpoising.

Once the airflow stabilises, the car regains downforce. The ride height then reduces again, creating a cycle of rocking back and forth, like a porpoise diving in and out of the sea. The name makes more sense now, doesn't it!

As the car gets faster, the ride height decreases disrupting the airflow below the car

!?!

Disrupted airflow creates a cycle making the car bounce up and down

SCAN TO WATCH THE VIDEO
SCAN TO WATCH THE VIDEO

On high-speed straights, the bouncing can heavily damage the floor and make the chassis unstable, whilst also impacting the car's ability to brake. It's also very uncomfortable for the drivers and some have even reported feeling seasick because of it.

Despite their simulations, teams didn't seem to anticipate this issue going into the season.

Unfortunately, porpoising is a problem that can never be accurately predicted on a team's simulator. Their windtunnel models also can't experience that downforce as they can't be run on a moving belt!

With the floor providing more downforce under the new regulations, the team's engineers want to keep the downforce as consistent as possible.

Over the course of the year, the teams were able to find solutions to reduce the cars from bouncing, but it wasn't an overnight fix! Even the FIA had to step in to help remedy the problem.

BAHRAIN

It was here. The start of a new era. Different regulations, some fresh (and unexpected) faces, plus a championship fight that was spicy from the very first race. What more could you want!

If you were a Ferrari fan, things started on a high in Bahrain. Charles Leclerc popped it on pole and secured victory at the first race of the season. Leclerc was so confident in his car, he even found time to joke on the penultimate lap that there was something strange with the engine - a nod to when he lost his maiden win at this same venue back in 2019 with power unit issues.

If only we knew what was to come...

Reliability issues were no laughing matter for the Red Bull Honda-powered cars though, as Pierre Gasly's race went up in flames (literally), as well as BOTH Max Verstappen and Sergio Perez being forced to end their races with just a few laps remaining. A nightmare start, especially for the reigning world champion.

Elsewhere on the grid, Kevin Magnussen made a stunning return to Haas after the departure of Nikita Mazepin, with K-Mag finishing his first race back in P5. Rookie Zhou Guanyu also scored points on his debut, with Lewis Hamilton finding himself on the podium alongside a Ferrari 1-2.

" FERRARI ARE BACK "

LAPS
57

CIRCUIT'S FIRST F1 RACE
2004

BAHRAIN INTERNATIONAL CIRCUIT
18 - 20 MAR 2022

10

LIGHTS OUT AND AWAY WE GO!

RETURN OF THE MAG

OMG SAMESIES, K-MAG

W **WTF1** @wtf1official
Hulkenberg will race for Aston Martin in Bahrain as Vettel tests positive for COVID-19

NICOOOOO.... HUUUUULKENBEERG!

RACE RUNDOWN

POINTS FOR ZHOU ON HIS DEBUT

LOVING THESE ON TRACK BATTLES ALREADY!

POS.	DRIVER
1	LECLERC
2	SAINZ
3	HAMILTON
4	RUSSELL
5	MAGNUSSEN
6	BOTTAS
7	OCON
8	TSUNODA
9	ALONSO
10	ZHOU
11	SCHUMACHER
12	STROLL
13	ALBON
14	RICCIARDO
15	NORRIS
16	LATIFI
17	HULKENBERG

NON FINISHERS

DNF	PEREZ
DNF	VERSTAPPEN
DNF	GASLY

FASTEST LAP
1:34.570
LECLERC

All aboard the
HYPE TRAIN

OH YES! THE HYPE IS REAL!

BUT MATT GOT SO EXCITED, HE MISSED HIS STOP! CAN YOU HELP HIM FIND HIS WAY TO THE FERRARI HYPE TRAIN?

FOLLOW THE RAILWAY LINES TO GET HIM BACK ON TRACK...

SOLUTIONS ON PAGE 116 - 117

SAUDI ARABIA

"ANOTHER BRILLIANT BATTLE!"

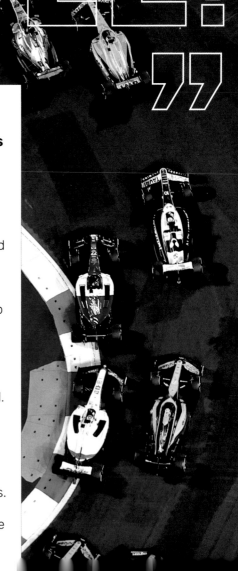

Fresh from the disappointment of Bahrain, Sergio Perez achieved his first pole position around the streets of Jeddah. Yuki Tsunoda's car couldn't take the start, so he joined a sore Mick Schumacher on the sidelines, after the Haas driver smashed his own car to pieces in qualifying.

Both the Alpines, in their special pink liveries, stole the show at the start of the race as Esteban Ocon and Fernando Alonso went wheel-to-wheel battling for sixth place. Shortly after, an early dummy pit call for Charles Leclerc made Perez box from the lead of the race, but moments later Nicholas Latifi found a wall to crash into and brought out a safety car. **#DeJaVu**

Perez was shafted, with it going from bad to worse when he was forced to give Carlos Sainz his third place, as it was decided Sainz was ahead of Perez when leaving the pit lane during the safety car period.

Chaos later followed, as a load of drivers broke down all within a few moments of each other, including Alonso, Daniel Ricciardo and Valtteri Bottas.

Sparks flew at the end of the race, with Max Verstappen fighting Leclerc for the win in the last laps. After a stunning and nail-biting series of DRS games, and some back and forth, Red Bull's Verstappen came out on top.

LAPS
50

CIRCUIT'S FIRST F1 RACE
2021

A MASSIVE IMPACT FOR MICK IN QUALIFYING

LATIFI HITS THE WALL!

PEREZ ON POLE!

ALONSO VS OCON

RACE RUNDOWN

LECLERC AND VERSTAPPEN BATTLE ON TRACK...

WTF1 @wtf1official
THEY'RE PLAYING DRS CHICKEN!!! WHAT!!! #SaudiArabianGP #WTF1

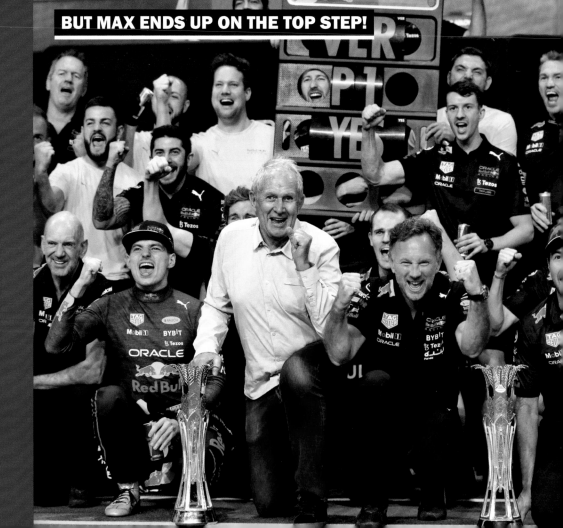

BUT MAX ENDS UP ON THE TOP STEP!

POS.	DRIVER
1	VERSTAPPEN
2	LECLERC
3	SAINZ
4	PEREZ
5	RUSSELL
6	OCON
7	NORRIS
8	GASLY
9	MAGNUSSEN
10	HAMILTON
11	ZHOU
12	HULKENBERG
13	STROLL

NON FINISHERS

DNF	ALBON
DNF	BOTTAS
DNF	ALONSO
DNF	RICCIARDO
DNF	LATIFI
DNS	TSUNODA
DNS	SCHUMACHER

FASTEST LAP
1:31.634
LECLERC

Tommy's Helmet Design Challenge

Each season, F1 drivers come out with new designs for their race helmets. But can you do any better?!

Sketch out your concept for an eye-catching race helmet!

Share your final designs with us using the hashtag #WTF1Annual

AUSTRALIA

" MORE VERSTAPPEN DRAMA "

F1 flew back Down Under, and delivered us a treat almost as good as Tim Tams.

Sebastian Vettel returned after missing the first two races with coronavirus, but probably wished he'd stayed at home a little while longer. As well as crashing out of FP3 and the race, he was slapped with a €5,000 fine for taking a scooter on the Albert Park track after FP1.

Whoops!

It was also a weekend to forget for Carlos Sainz who qualified a disappointing ninth in a pole-winning car, and also managed to beach his Ferrari in the gravel on just the second lap of the race. Quite the contrast to his teammate, Charles Leclerc, who put on a dominant display securing pole, leading every lap as well as achieving the fastest lap and then winning by more than 20 seconds - a grand slam!

His victory was made all the sweeter as his championship rival, Max Verstappen, was forced to retire with yet another fuel system issue, his second failure in three races.

Leclerc left Australia with 71 points, 34 points clear of George Russell who sat second in the drivers' championship. Verstappen, with two DNFs to his name, had just 25 points and a lot of catching up to do.

LAPS
58

CIRCUIT'S FIRST F1 RACE
1996

IT'S AMAZING TO BE BACK IN ALBERT PARK!

DANNY RIC - HOME HERO

SCOOTER SEB

 Matt Gallagher @MattyWTF1
Danny Ric was on great form this weekend,
great to see him smile and enjoy himself 😍

 19

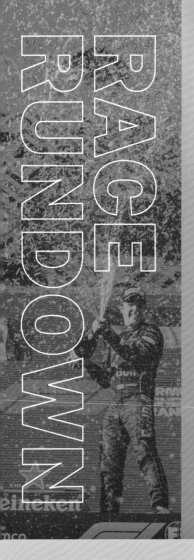

TWO DNFS ALREADY FOR VERSTAPPEN... NOT IDEAL!

POS.	DRIVER
1	LECLERC
2	PEREZ
3	RUSSELL
4	HAMILTON
5	NORRIS
6	RICCIARDO
7	OCON
8	BOTTAS
9	GASLY
10	ALBON
11	ZHOU
12	STROLL
13	SCHUMACHER
14	MAGNUSSEN
15	TSUNODA
16	LATIFI
17	ALONSO

NON FINISHERS

DNF	VERSTAPPEN
DNF	VETTEL
DNF	SAINZ

FASTEST LAP
1:20.260
LECLERC

RUSSELL AND NORRIS GO WHEEL TO WHEEL!

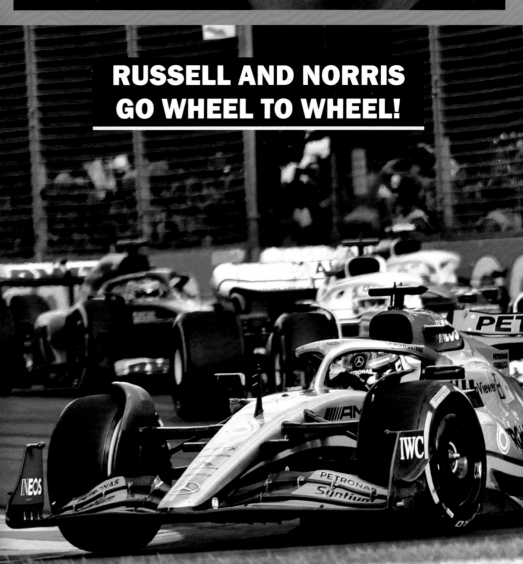

LECLERC WINS DOWN UNDER!

Alex Albon managed something not seen in over a decade at the 2022 Australian Grand Prix! Behind the wheel of his Williams, Albon made his tyres last the distance of the race, only pitting on the final lap to stop himself being disqualified for not using two tyre compounds during the grand prix.

The set of hard tyres lasted an incredible 57 laps, with Albon switching to a set of softs on the last lap. He even managed to finish the race in tenth, securing his, and Williams', first championship point of the season!

Having started P20, Albon managed to make his way up the grid during the 58-lap race. After two safety cars, and plenty of chaos, he found himself in seventh before pitting and eventually earning himself a top-10 finish.

This season, F1's tyre supplier Pirelli introduced a new 18-inch tyre. The tyres might be heavier and larger in size, but they're designed to reduce overheating and be less prone to degradation which Alex certainly proved to be the case!

There are five 'slick' compounds that Pirelli can pick from for each event. Of the five, they'll choose the three most appropriate compounds which will make up the hard, medium and soft tyres available to teams.

F101

WE KNOW WHEEL

A GUIDE TO TYRES IN F1

HARD

The firmest of the three compounds. These tyres have the longest life, so are great for a long stint during the race. They also provide the least amount of grip and are used at circuits that might have unusually high track temperatures or rougher surfaces.

MEDIUM

You've guessed it, the medium tyre is somewhere between the hard and the soft compound. A great compromise, which is slower than the softs but will last longer than them, and faster than the hards but doesn't last as long.

SOFT

These compounds will help you set the fastest times, so are a popular choice during qualifying stints. They're commonly used at street circuits or tracks with a nice smooth surface, but are also the quickest tyre to degrade so will only be at their best for a short window.

WET TYRES

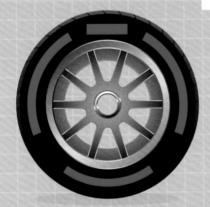
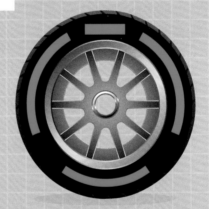

INTERMEDIATE

Teams will bring out these tyres if there's a wet track with no standing water, or if the circuit is starting to dry. They're a versatile compound, and can even be worn down into an 'inter-slick' compound which takes a driver from a wet to dry tyre with no need to stop.

EXTREME WET

Designed for heavy rain, these tyres can disperse a big amount of water and help the cars grip to the track surface when wet. Generally, drivers aren't the biggest fans of these tyres, as they're very hard, and will switch to the inters at the earliest opportunity!

EMILIA ROMAGNA

"LECLERC SLIPS UP"

LAPS
63

CIRCUIT'S FIRST F1 RACE
1980

The first Sprint race of the year undid some of the chaos that had occurred from a last-minute downpour during Imola qualifying. Nevertheless, it was still a Max Verstappen and Charles Leclerc front row on race day. Tasty 🍿

Verstappen got a great start in the damp conditions, with Lando Norris delivering another wet weather masterclass to jump both Ferraris and get into third. Unfortunately for Carlos Sainz, his destiny once again lay in a gravel trap as contact with Daniel Ricciardo meant he was beached and his race over before it really began.

Leclerc managed to pass the quick-starting Norris and get into third place, where he stayed for most of the race. That was until he launched his Ferrari over a sausage kerb, losing control of his car and ending up in a nearby barrier. He was able to get going again after the mistake, but required a front wing change and would only be able to climb back up to sixth place.

Norris gladly accepted the promotion to a podium as a result of Leclerc's error and joined Red Bull in their first 1-2 result of the season.

THE FIRST SPRINT OF THE SEASON

MAX GETS A GREAT START

FIRST LAP CHAOS!

DANNY RIC SENDS SAINZ SPINNING OFF!

WTF1 @wtf1official
Lando Norris has scored a podium in the last three Italian F1 races 🥈🏆

POS.	DRIVER
1	VERSTAPPEN
2	PEREZ
3	NORRIS
4	RUSSELL
5	BOTTAS
6	LECLERC
7	TSUNODA
8	VETTEL
9	MAGNUSSEN
10	STROLL
11	ALBON
12	GASLY
13	HAMILTON
14	OCON
15	ZHOU
16	LATIFI
17	SCHUMACHER
18	RICCIARDO
19	ALONSO

NON FINISHERS

DNF	SAINZ

26

FASTEST LAP
1:18.446
VERSTAPPEN

CONNECT THE DOTS
WITH GUENTHER STEINER

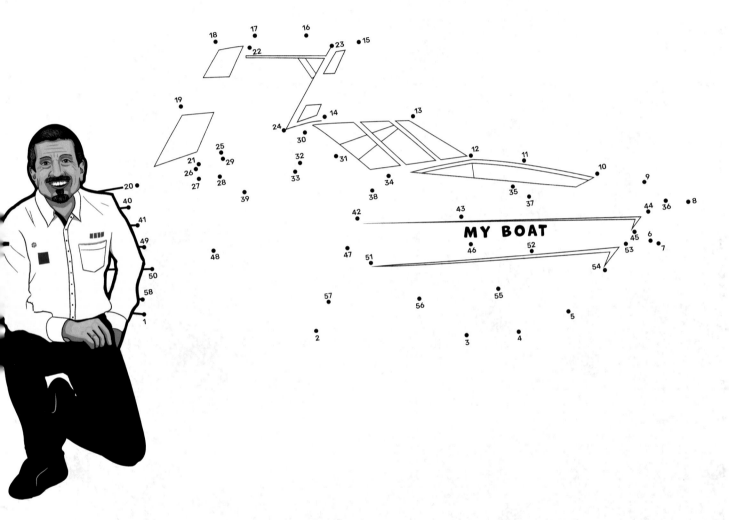

MY BOAT

GUENTHER STEINER HAS A BIG SMILE ON HIS FACE,
AFTER A SOLID START FOR HAAS WITH POINTS
SCORED IN THREE OUT OF FOUR RACES
AT THE START OF THE SEASON.

JOIN THE DOTS TO HELP HIM REVEAL THE
LATEST UPGRADE TO THE STEINER SHIP...

MIAMI

LAPS
57

CIRCUIT'S
FIRST F1
RACE
2022

Welcome to Miami, F1.

The championship's first visit to the city in Florida had almost as many celebrities as it did overtakes, it's just a shame TV direction didn't show us much of the latter.

The Ferrari lads secured a front-row lockout, but it took only seconds for Max Verstappen to disturb that as he darted past Carlos Sainz to sneak into second place. Leclerc's lead was also short-lived, as Verstappen stormed past with DRS at the start of lap 9. He'd stay there for the entirety of the race, apart from when he had to pit, and go on to take his third win of the season.

Elsewhere, Pierre Gasly sustained damage from an incident with Fernando Alonso which led to him making contact with Lando Norris laps later. An innocent Norris was sent into a series of spins and lost his right-rear tyre in the process, which triggered a safety car.

When we got back racing, Mick Schumacher looked on course for his first championship points. However, he clashed with his paddock bestie, Sebastian Vettel, in the final moments of the race.

Not the finest moment for **#TeamSmick.**

The top three took a whacky police escort to the podium, which probably took the same time needed to fill the fake harbour with *actual* water.

"THAT WAS WEIRD"

IT'S BEHIND YOU!

ANYONE FANCY A DIP?

Katy Fairman @katyfairman
How many bodyguards do you think Martin Brundle will have to deal with on the Miami track walk later 😂 #MiamiGP

AMAZING EFFORT ON THIS FAN OUTFIT

BRING IT.

SOME AMAZING ONE-OFF HELMET DESIGNS

MICK AND YUKI FIGHT FOR POSITION

POS.	DRIVER
1	VERSTAPPEN
2	LECLERC
3	SAINZ
4	PEREZ
5	RUSSELL
6	HAMILTON
7	BOTTAS
8	OCON
9	ALBON
10	STROLL
11	ALONSO
12	TSUNODA
13	RICCIARDO
14	LATIFI
15	SCHUMACHER

NON FINISHERS

DNF	MAGNUSSEN
DNF	VETTEL
DNF	GASLY
DNF	NORRIS
DNF	ZHOU

FASTEST LAP
1:31.361
VERSTAPPEN

Welcome to Miami!

Matt's DIARY

MIAMI GP

Meeting F1 fans around the city

Ah, Miami. What a trip this was. I always get excited when an opportunity comes up to go abroad and do some fun F1 stuff (can't really believe this is my job!).

Day 1

We arrived in Miami and immediately set off for South Beach as that's where a lot of awesome F1 activations were taking place. We went to a DHL pop up which had an F1 car literally on the beach and whilst there, was lucky enough to interview Romain Grosjean for a few minutes too. After this we roamed around the area and found the Williams F1 pop up store which again had an F1 car in it. It was really cool to see how many people were taking an interest in the sport!

Day 2

The big day. Filming with Charles Leclerc for the very first time on the WTF1 YouTube channel. We did a hilarious 'You Steer, I Drive' challenge where one of us was steering the F1 car and the other was controlling the pedals. Safe to say it was absolute carnage!! We only had 12 minutes with him to film absolutely everything and it's definitely one of my favourite videos.

Day 3

We went to a McLaren event in the evening where I managed to very briefly see Lando and Danny! Lando shouted 'oh my God it's Matt Gallagher' and then gave me a hug, Danny saw me late but then the face he made when looking back at me... I'll never forget that!! It's true love.

Day 4

Going to the Miami GP track!! It was so awesome to meet so many of you and also experience what a 'new age' F1 circuit looks like. The fan experience was great, seeing the fake marina in the flesh was quite something to behold but I'll never forget having to pay $6 for a bottle of water...

Day 5

I was lucky enough to be back at the track on the Saturday as well, filmed some crazy TikTok's including an F1 car floating on water and met lots more of you too which was easily my favourite part of the day.

Day 6

We weren't at the track for Sunday as we needed to film one of our most popular series 'The Internet's Best Reactions'. So where better to watch it than on the beach!! We went to a festival called FTX Off The Grid which had loads of cool cars, F1 bits and bobs, and music acts in the evening. Overall, it was an incredible experience and one that I will definitely never forget!

It was so good to see Danny Ric last night 😢

SCAN TO WATCH THE VIDEO

Filming with Charles Leclerc!

31

CAN KATY SURVIVE HER FIRST TIME KARTING?

**DAYTONA
SANDOWN PARK
UNITED KINGDOM**

KATY FAIRMAN

AGE: **26**

EXPERIENCE: **0**

DRIVING LESSONS: **25**

BOOKS WRITTEN: **1**

FAVOURITE DRIVER:
NICO ROSBERG

SODIKART
RT8

the author
^

KATY FAIRMAN MIGHT SET THE
FASTEST TIMES WRITING ARTICLES
FOR WTF1.COM, BUT SHE HAS
NEVER BEEN KARTING BEFORE.

UNTIL NOW!

SO KATY, HOW DID YOU DO?

SEND IT!

REGRETS?

REGRETS.

As someone who isn't very good at putting themselves out of their comfort zone, this challenge was pretty nerve wracking for me. It had been raining in the morning, so the track was damp in patches but fortunately had mainly dried when I headed out for my first taste of the circuit. They were never going to be lap records, but it was good to get a feeling for the kart, oh and realise that I had a brake pedal. Whoops!

From my first lap to my fifth lap, I shaved off 30 seconds with my quickest time so far being...

1.04.300

Going out there on my own was good, but I needed a mentor to help and guide me if I wanted to improve my times. So, who better than W Series legend **ALICE POWELL**!

Alice talked me through my best attempt, showing me where to improve and then we both headed out on track to try and find the best racing lines. She gave me a time to beat, under 60 seconds. No pressure, Katy!

Things seemed to be going well, until I lost control and spun right in front of her. Absolutely mortifying. After picking up my damaged ego, I tried another few laps and could certainly notice an improvement. Even Alice was impressed, and was sure it wasn't my first time karting. I'll definitely take that. My new best time?

0.58.724

I was getting quicker but Alice wasn't finished yet. I now had a new target; under 56 seconds.

For my last run, I headed out on my own. Trying to remember all my training, I gave it everything. There was still the odd mistake, and a VERY close call with a tyre barrier, but generally most of my laps seemed decent. Still, I didn't think it was enough! However, after what felt like a lifetime, Matt finally told me my fastest lap time...

0.55.334

I'd done it, and by seven tenths too. I was overjoyed and actually really proud of how much I'd learnt in just a few laps thanks to the help of Alice and the team at Daytona!

REVIEWING THE LAPS

SCAN TO WATCH THE VIDEO

SPAIN

"HEARTBREAK FOR CHARLES"

Our two title protagonists lined up on the front row once again, with Charles Leclerc keeping Max Verstappen behind him as Charles led from pole.

Behind them, Kevin Magnussen and Lewis Hamilton got their elbows out, with the Haas driver finding himself speeding through the gravel on the first lap.

Not one to miss out, Carlos Sainz was once again reunited with a gravel trap for the third time in four races but avoided beaching his Ferrari and managed to crawl out. In a shocking twist, Verstappen did just the same only laps later!

With his championship rival now down in fourth, and having topped every session over the weekend, this seemed like an easy victory for Leclerc. Then disaster struck, and we all witnessed the first sign of trouble at Ferrari: Charles' engine failed.

Up until Spain, Ferrari seemed almost bulletproof compared to Red Bull. Both teams were quick, but Verstappen had already taken two retirements this season as a result of his car's unreliability. Ferrari had the upper hand, but could that all be about to change?

Despite his journey through the gravel and battling DRS issues during the race, Verstappen was ordered past Sergio Perez. Max also overtook George Russell to secure another win and found himself now leading the drivers' standings for the first time in 2022.

LAPS
66

CIRCUIT'S FIRST F1 RACE
1991

MATTIA BINOTTO TRIES TO ORDER TWO CANS OF RED BULL FROM CHRISTIAN HORNER

BEAUTIFUL OVERHEAD VIEW OF THE FINAL SECTOR

LOCAL HERO SALUTES HIS FANS

RACE RUNDOWN

WTF1 @wtf1official
WOW THAT A BATTLE BETWEEN VERSTAPPEN AND RUSSELL!
#SpanishGP #WTF1

POS.	DRIVER
1	VERSTAPPEN
2	PEREZ
3	RUSSELL
4	SAINZ
5	HAMILTON
6	BOTTAS
7	OCON
8	NORRIS
9	ALONSO
10	TSUNODA
11	VETTEL
12	RICCIARDO
13	GASLY
14	SCHUMACHER
15	STROLL
16	LATIFI
17	MAGNUSSEN
18	ALBON

NON FINISHERS

DNF	ZHOU
DNF	LECLERC

FASTEST LAP
1:24.108
PEREZ

GEORGE RUSSELL IS THE TYPE OF GUY TO END UP ON THE PODIUM

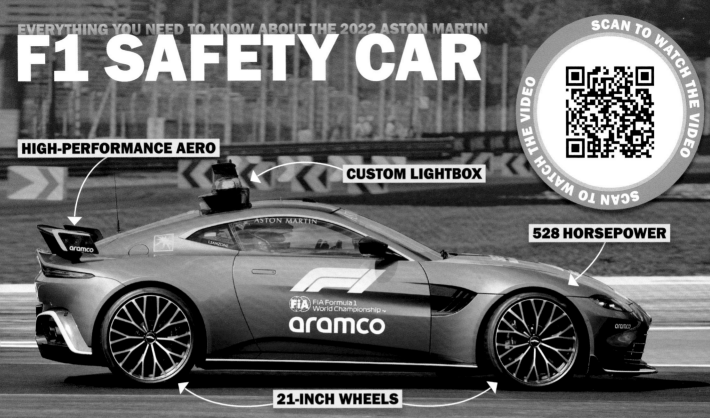

F1 SAFETY CAR

SCAN TO WATCH THE VIDEO

HIGH-PERFORMANCE AERO

CUSTOM LIGHTBOX

528 HORSEPOWER

21-INCH WHEELS

Outside of the F1 cars, this is one of the other stars that can be seen on track over a race weekend. Matt had a chat with Andy Curtis (Head of Performance Driving at Aston Martin) who talked him through their 2022 F1 Safety Car.

AC: "This is **one of three** safety cars that Aston Martin supplies to the F1 calendar for the year. We have to put a certain amount of kilometres on each car before it's being signed off as fit for purpose for F1 to use out on the circuit.

"This Aston Martin safety car is based on the **V8 F1 Edition V12 Vantage**. This car is beefed up on the suspension to take the extra weight of the amount of support kit that we have to put into the car.

"To help with performance, the **aero kit** is similar to the F1 Edition Vantage, but not identical; it had to be upgraded to take on the extra weight and increased downforce required to lead the F1 pack around the circuit, meaning that the rear wing, diffuser and side skirts are all slightly larger.

"The **lightbox** was custom developed and designed by the Aston Martin in-house design team. We had to work out a system of how it was going to be bonded to the roof, to ensure that it does not disrupt the airflow and stays securely attached when the car is going around each track at high speed.

"The person sitting in the passenger seat (Richard Darker) is the main point of contact to Race Control. They have a number of **data screens** which display key info sent through to the car, which Richard absorbs before feeding back to Bernd Mayländer (safety car driver), so that he can be totally focused on driving.

"Whilst fans at home or indeed the drivers may think that the safety car isn't going quick enough when leading the pack, it is very much acting under instruction from the Race Director and Race Control. Otherwise we would and could go much quicker!"

MATT MEETS ANDY CURTIS, HEAD OF PERFORMANCE DRIVING

THAT ENGINE NOISE, THOUGH

37

MONACO

"WET MONACO MADNESS"

They say racing in Monaco is like trying to ride your bike around your living room. So when you get a last-minute downpour before lights out, you know it's going to be a challenge.

After a long delay, racing got underway with Leclerc managing to stay out of trouble. He led from pole and was finally in with a chance of breaking his home race 'curse'.

With this being the first time the circuit was wet all weekend, chaos ensued. As well as Nicholas Latifi managing one of the slowest crashes we've ever seen at the famous hairpin, Lewis Hamilton and Esteban Ocon played a very expensive game of bumper cars around the principality.

Several midfield cars also switched to intermediates as the race got going, showing the potential of the tyre. Soon the frontrunners wanted to try it, with Sergio Perez being the first, closely followed by Leclerc from the lead. However, Charles' teammate, Carlos Sainz, stayed out a few more laps and gambled by going on to slicks.

At the same time Carlos pitted for dry tyres, Charles also arrived in the pit lane. "Stay out, stay out," Ferrari radioed to Leclerc but it was too late. The team was then forced to try a messy double-stack. It was a disaster for Leclerc, who came out fourth as Red Bull also competed a successful back-to-back stop with both their drivers.

Perez led with the top four separated by just seconds, but the race soon came to a halt after Mick Schumacher demolished his Haas and brought out the red flags - his second big shunt in just a matter of races.

After a rolling safety car restart, Perez managed to hold on to his first place and secured victory around Monaco!

LAPS
64

CIRCUIT'S FIRST F1 RACE
1950

WAIT, THIS ISN'T THE SWIMMING POOL SECTION

ANOTHER EXPENSIVE CRASH FOR MICK

WEATHERMAN SEB

RACE RUNDOWN

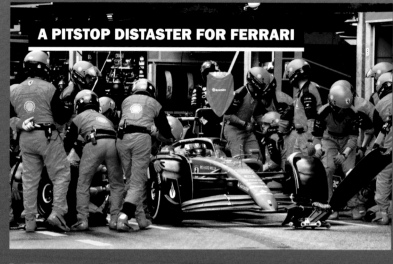

A PITSTOP DISTASTER FOR FERRARI

IT'S ALL GETTING A BIT FEISTY BETWEEN HAMILTON AND OCON

POS.	DRIVER
1	PEREZ
2	SAINZ
3	VERSTAPPEN
4	LECLERC
5	RUSSELL
6	NORRIS
7	ALONSO
8	HAMILTON
9	BOTTAS
10	VETTEL
11	GASLY
12	OCON
13	RICCIARDO
14	STROLL
15	LATIFI
16	ZHOU
17	TSUNODA

NON FINISHERS

DNF	ALBON
DNF	SCHUMACHER
DNF	MAGNUSSEN

FASTEST LAP
1:14.693
NORRIS

WINNERS

AZERBAIJAN

It was once again pole position for Charles Leclerc, but a different Red Bull lined up alongside him around the Azerbaijan street circuit.

Fresh from his win in Monaco, Perez found himself on the front row and ready to secure his second consecutive win at the Baku track. Things started well for the Mexican, as Charles suffered a lock up at Turn 1 allowing Perez straight through.

Only a few laps later, disaster struck for Carlos Sainz as his Ferrari conked out as a result of a hydraulics failure. Teammate Leclerc made use of the Virtual Safety Car that was deployed, pitting for a fresh set of hard tyres. Despite it being a slow stop, the undercut worked and Leclerc would go on to lead the race, but not for long.

Speeding down the start/finish straight, smoke started to pour out the back of Leclerc's Ferrari as he experienced ANOTHER power unit failure. In just a matter of weeks, it had gone from Verstappen being on the back foot after two DNFs to now Leclerc being the vulnerable one in the championship battle.

Verstappen became the sixth different winner around the Baku circuit, with Red Bull managing to lock in another 1-2 result on a day that Ferrari fans would wish to forget.

"NIGHTMARE FOR FERRARI"

LAPS
51

CIRCUIT'S FIRST F1 RACE
2016

BAKU CITY CIRCUIT
10 - 12 JUN 2022

42

BACK IN BAKU

WELL THAT'S A NEW ONE!

WHEN SOMEONE SPOILS THE RACE RESULTS FOR YOU

HATS OFF TO ALONSO

RACE RUNDOWN

MAX ENDED HIS BAKU JINX TO BECOME ITS SIXTH DIFFERENT WINNER

DOMINANT FROM RED BULL

POS.	DRIVER
1	VERSTAPPEN
2	PEREZ
3	RUSSELL
4	HAMILTON
5	GASLY
6	VETTEL
7	ALONSO
8	RICCIARDO
9	NORRIS
10	OCON
11	BOTTAS
12	ALBON
13	TSUNODA
14	SCHUMACHER
15	LATIFI

NON FINISHERS

DNF	STROLL
DNF	MAGNUSSEN
DNF	ZHOU
DNF	LECLERC
DNF	SAINZ

44

FASTEST LAP
1:46.046
PEREZ

wtf1-to-1.
WITH SEBASTIAN VETTEL

Everybody is a Sebastian Vettel fan, so naturally we FREAKED out when offered the chance to chat to the four-time F1 champion earlier this year.

WHAT'S THE CRAZIEST VICTORY PARTY YOU'VE EVER HAD?

Well, it must be a while ago!

End of 2013 we had a really strong end to the season and I was able to secure the title with some races to go.

Every Sunday the last few races were good, so it was like a sequence of parties.

WHAT'S ONE RULE YOU WOULD CHANGE IN F1 IF YOU COULD?

Track limits.

Sometimes the discussions are very silly about track limits, so maybe simplify that. I would also be happy if I was allowed to touch other people's cars and not get fined a massive amount of money...

YOU'RE THE ONLY F1 DRIVER WHO IS NOT ON SOCIAL MEDIA. WILL WE EVER SEE A SEBASTIAN VETTEL SOCIAL ACCOUNT?

I feel really lonely. I don't know, I never started it and I am quite happy. I also don't have the apps. I'm busy enough with my phone and trying to not use it too much. I find when somebody shows me something on their phone, it's really interesting. You just keep going up, going up and there's more and more. So I'm quite defensive in terms of installing social media because

I can see why people are, I don't want to say addicted in a bad way, but why people are spending so much time on there.

TURN TO PAGE 70 TO FIND OUT WHAT HAPPENED WHEN SEB FINALLY CREATED @SEBASTIANVETTEL

DO YOU THINK F1 SHOULD GO FULLY ELECTRIC?

I think right now, no. I think the demands are very different, from what I understand, to say your electric car and a Formula 1 car if it was electric. Like Formula E basically just with more power for F1.

I don't think that it would be a great contribution to the world, because the cells that you develop would be just useless for what you need. But I do think F1 needs to be open to take on the responsibility that we all have of holding on to things that we learn to enjoy and love, and the passions we've got. F1 can contribute to making the world a better place.

It sounds very romantic, but I think using the engineering power, all the clever minds thinking of solutions, should be used and translated for something that benefits all of us in the future.

SCAN TO WATCH THE VIDEO

CANADA

Fernando Alonso ended the tradition of having Red Bulls or Ferraris on the front row with a qualifying masterclass, popping his Alpine into second place for race day. El plan in action, for now.

Max Verstappen and Carlos Sainz both battled for the race win with a two-stop strategy, each benefitting from safety car interventions on separate occasions. Max snuck in an early stop as a result of his teammate Sergio Perez's misfortune, whereas Sainz took advantage of Yuki Tsunoda driving into the barriers after his stop, with cold tyres likely to blame.

When Sainz exited the pit lane during the safety car period, he was on Verstappen's tail with fresher tyres and a new-spec rear wing. It was game on, but despite Sainz's best efforts, Verstappen clung on to claim his sixth grand prix victory of the season.

Desperate to keep his championship hopes alive, Charles Leclerc delivered a strong recovery drive to go from the back of the grid, thanks to engine penalties, to finish fifth. Alonso, on the other hand, failed to keep his second-place start position and eventually finished ninth after an air leak developed on his engine and he received a post-race penalty for weaving.

LAPS
70

CIRCUIT'S FIRST F1 RACE
1978

"VERSTAPPEN TOO GOOD"

41 AND STILL RAPID

EL PLANADA

RACE RUNDOWN

@DUDEWITHSIGN

GREAT RECOVERY DRIVE

POS.	DRIVER
1	VERSTAPPEN
2	SAINZ
3	HAMILTON
4	RUSSELL
5	LECLERC
6	OCON
7	BOTTAS
8	ZHOU
9	ALONSO
10	STROLL
11	RICCIARDO
12	VETTEL
13	ALBON
14	GASLY
15	NORRIS
16	LATIFI
17	MAGNUSSEN

NON FINISHERS

DNF	TSUNODA
DNF	SCHUMACHER
DNF	PEREZ

Matt Gallagher @MattyWTF1
What a fantastic race between Verstappen and
Sainz!! That was heart in your mouth stuff!

48

FASTEST LAP
1:15.749
SAINZ

1

2

3

ZERO P ZERO

4

5

6

7

Salut Gilles
8

GUESS THE CIRCUIT

CAN YOU IDENTIFY THESE EIGHT CIRCUITS FROM ACROSS THE GLOBE?

49

ANSWERS ON PAGE 116 - 117

GREAT BRITAIN

As well as the WTF1 Clubhouse for company, Silverstone delivered one of the best races on the calendar... no British bias here. Promise.

Carlos Sainz locked in his maiden pole position, and was ready to convert it into his first F1 victory. However, a huge accident involving Zhou Guanyu meant the race was almost immediately red flagged.

After contact with George Russell, Zhou's Alfa Romeo was dramatically flipped upside down before skidding across the track and ending up behind a tyre barrier. Alex Albon was also punted into a wall on the pit straight. Both drivers were taken to hospital but were thankfully fine 🙏

When the race restarted, Carlos and Max Verstappen fought for the lead with everyone getting their elbows out. Early contact between Charles Leclerc and Sergio Perez resulted in the Mexican pitting for a new front wing which dropped him to last.

A costly mistake from Sainz allowed Verstappen to snatch the lead, but it was short-lived as his Red Bull was damaged after running over a piece of carbon fibre. With his title rival now limping around the track, Leclerc needed to get past Sainz. Ferrari were slow to organise team orders, despite Charles being faster, but he did eventually overtake Sainz for first place.

Suddenly, Esteban Ocon stopped on track and brought out a safety car. Ferrari boxed Sainz for soft tyres, but left Charles out on old hards. ***Why did they not pit Leclerc?!***

Carlos soon caught up to his teammate, who couldn't keep him back on older tyres. Poor Leclerc then tried to hold up Perez, with the two displaying some epic racing, before home hero Lewis Hamilton snuck through while they were battling for position.

Sainz achieved his maiden victory, with Perez coming from last to second to join Hamilton on the iconic podium.

"AN INSTANT CLASSIC"

**LAPS
52**

**CIRCUIT'S
FIRST F1
RACE
1950**

WHO WORE IT BETTER?

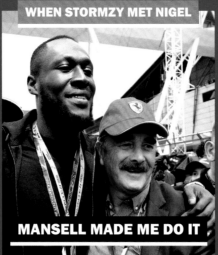

WHEN STORMZY MET NIGEL

MANSELL MADE ME DO IT

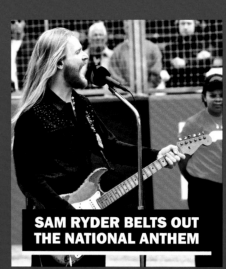

SAM RYDER BELTS OUT THE NATIONAL ANTHEM

YIKES!

FORTUNATELY ZHOU WAS UNHARMED IN THIS SCARY CRASH

WHEEL-TO-WHEEL RACING ALL ROUND!

RACE RUNDOWN

AN ICONIC HERO, UNIVERSALLY LOVED ACROSS THE WORLD...

STANDS NEXT TO TOM CRUISE

CHECO'S DAD ANTONIO PEREZ ENJOYING HIS SON'S P2 FINISH

NATIONAL CHAIR OF THE BRITISH MOTORSPORTS MARSHAL'S CLUB NADINE LEWIS PRESENTS SERGIO PEREZ WITH HIS 2ND PLACE TROPHY

POS.	DRIVER
1	SAINZ
2	PEREZ
3	HAMILTON
4	LECLERC
5	ALONSO
6	NORRIS
7	VERSTAPPEN
8	SCHUMACHER
9	VETTEL
10	MAGNUSSEN
11	STROLL
12	LATIFI
13	RICCIARDO
14	TSUNODA

NON FINISHERS

DNF	OCON
DNF	GASLY
DNF	BOTTAS
DNF	RUSSELL
DNF	ZHOU
DNF	ALBON

WTF1 @wtf1official
Seb congratulating Mick on his first points 🥹 #BritishGP #WTF1

52

FASTEST LAP
1:30.510
HAMILTON

THERE'S ALWAYS LOVE FOR LEWIS AT SILVERSTONE

GEORGINA OUTSIDE THE ICONIC SILVERSTONE WING

EDVARDAS AND GIEDRĖ ON THE WELLINGTON STRAIGHT

TEAM

wtf1.

FAN CAM
AT SILVERSTONE

As well as getting to enjoy the WTF1 Clubhouse, our Team WTF1 Members shared snaps of their experiences from Silverstone this year.

CHRIS AND HIS FATHER-IN-LAW STEVE CHECK OUT THE HAMILTON STRAIGHT

LAUREN, JOSH, NATALIE AND TOM ENJOY THE MAIN STAGE

JORDAN & LINDSAY SOAK UP THE ATMOSPHERE (LITERALLY)

TASIA AND ADAM MEET ESTIE BESTIE HIMSELF

AMAZING WORK BY HEATHER WEARING HER WTF1 MERCH AND GETTING SOME LOVE FROM YUKI TSUNODA IN RETURN!

TAMRYN WAS LUCKY ENOUGH TO ACTUALLY GO INSIDE THE MCLAREN PIT GARAGE!

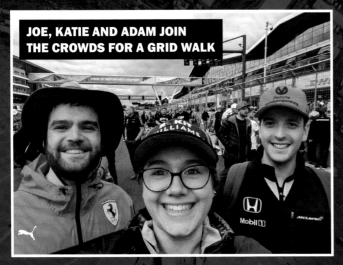

JOE, KATIE AND ADAM JOIN THE CROWDS FOR A GRID WALK

MOLLY & STEPHEN WAITING FOR THE RACE TO BEGIN!

ADAM & KENNEDY AT LUFFIELD CORNER

KATIE & LUCY EXPERIENCING THE FULL RANGE OF WEATHER CONDITIONS IN A TRADITIONAL BRITISH SUMMER

team wtf1.
clubhouse
at the British GP 2022

We were back again for another incredible weekend at WTF1 Clubhouse!

On the grounds of Whittlebury Park and only 15 minutes walk to the track, Team WTF1 members enjoyed a whole host of entertainment, special guests, competitions, our own fake marina (bring it, Miami!) and top quality food with a licensed bar.

www.wtf1.com

@wtf1official

@wtf1official

/wtf1official

wtf1official

Katy & Tommy recorded a live podcast with our special guest, 3-time W Series Champion **JAMIE CHADWICK** who also got a ride in our amazing hot air balloon!

ROW 5
VETTEL WAY

Tommy got involved with the games in an epic cornhole battle!

borrowed

Matt ~~stole~~ the buggy used for Team WTF1 circuit transfers, so that he could track down fellow campers to test their knowledge on their favourite F1 teams!

Ryan & Co head to the track!

Chantelle-Emma chills out by the big WTF1 tent

Sean grabs a selfie with Matt & Katy!

Alex & XXX check out the WTF1 Marina!

If you are interested in joining us for future WTF1 Clubhouse events, check out wtf1.com/clubhouse to find out more

Silverstone Marina

AUSTRIA

Orange flare smoke billowed out of the grandstands as Max Verstappen set off from pole.

Carlos Sainz and George Russell had a little moment on the first lap, but it was Sergio Perez who found himself the victim of the notorious Turn 4 gravel trap thanks to Russell who got a five-second penalty for the offence.

The race was packed with overtakes and action, including an excellent battle between Lewis Hamilton and both Haas cars - who'd have thought we'd be saying that after last year!

Up at the front, Leclerc was on another level and managed to sneak up the inside of Verstappen to take the lead of the race, something he'd go on to do another two times over the grand prix.

It even looked like his teammate Sainz would be able to pass Verstappen to make it a Ferrari 1-2, but his engine went bang. Forced to park his wounded Ferrari on a hill, the car suddenly became engulfed in flames as Carlos clambered out.

Unlike his teammate, who suffered his fourth DNF of the season so far, Leclerc reached the chequered flag to win his first race since Australia. Verstappen finished just behind in second with Hamilton completing the podium trio.

LAPS
71

CIRCUIT'S FIRST F1 RACE 1970

" WHAT **LECLERC** NEEDED "

TELL ME IT'S HILLY WITHOUT TELLING ME IT'S HILLY...

MAX WINS THE SPRINT

THE HILLS ARE ALIVE WITH THE SOUND OF "MAX, MAX, MAX, SUPER MAX MAX..."

GASLY SPINS OUT!

MUY CALIENTE!

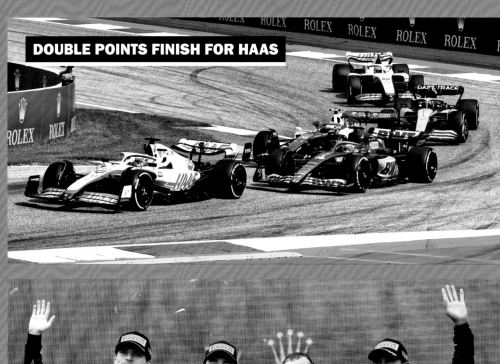

DOUBLE POINTS FINISH FOR HAAS

POS.	DRIVER
1	LECLERC
2	VERSTAPPEN
3	HAMILTON
4	RUSSELL
5	OCON
6	SCHUMACHER
7	NORRIS
8	MAGNUSSEN
9	RICCIARDO
10	ALONSO
11	BOTTAS
12	ALBON
13	STROLL
14	ZHOU
15	GASLY
16	TSUNODA
17	VETTEL

NON FINISHERS

DNF	SAINZ
DNF	LATIFI
DNF	PEREZ

Katy Fairman @katyfairman
Absolutely buzzing for Charles! Well doneee 🏆👏
#AustrianGP

60

FASTEST LAP
1:07.275
VERSTAPPEN

F1 01

WHY DON'T F1 CARS HAVE A HANDBRAKE?

There was a very sketchy moment during the Austrian Grand Prix, when Carlos Sainz was forced to park his Ferrari on a hill whilst it was on fire. The car rolled back, with Sainz still trying to leap out, and left many questioning if F1 cars have handbrakes.

Well, the short answer is no, and here's why.

SCAN TO WATCH THE VIDEO

It's no secret that weight is a big thing in F1. The lighter the car, the faster you'll likely go. This means teams will strip back on non-essential things, such as an easy-to-use reverse gear or a handbrake, to save some valuable kilograms.

For Sainz, the lack of handbrake wasn't really the issue. Yes, seeing him roll down the hill resulted in us having our hearts in our mouths for a brief moment, but those on the sidelines should have been better prepared for the situation.

Ideally, marshals would have been on the scene much quicker, with wedges to stop the car rolling back and the relevant fire extinguishers for the flames. It was reported after the event that something was placed under the Ferrari tyre, but it rolled over it.

Not something you would expect from the 'pinnacle of motorsport', is it? Especially as the marshal post was situated on the hill at Turn 4, so it can't come as a surprise that cars might roll back down towards the track!

So, what does a car do if it needs to stop on a hill without a handbrake? Usually, F1 drivers will stay in gear to ensure they don't roll back, but of course if your car is on fire you're probably wanting to get out as soon as possible.

It's all a balancing act, but no, they are not grabbing a big old handbrake stick and kicking the rear end out.

It was a lucky escape for Carlos though, with his car looking pretty charred afterwards. As ever, we're also so grateful for all the wonderful and brave work marshals in motorsport do.

FRANCE

Continuing the momentum from Austria, Charles Leclerc started from pole and despite Max Verstappen giving it his best shot to pass for the lead, Leclerc held on to first place.

But then came the self-confessed mistake that would later define Leclerc's 2022 championship hopes; he crashed while leading the race and it was game over.

The Ferrari was stuck in the barriers, and although Charles was unhurt, the scream he let out on the team radio let everyone know that this was a big moment in the fight for the title.

Ferrari then bottled the strategy on their one remaining car. First they gave Carlos Sainz a five-second penalty for an unsafe release, before calling him into the pits when he was in the middle of a fight with Sergio Perez for third place - were they not watching the race!? Finally, he served a 9.3s stop just ten laps from the end which seemed to prevent him fighting for a likely podium finish.

During the final laps, George Russell clonked his Mercedes into Sergio Perez's Red Bull, with Zhou Guanyu breaking down moments later causing the virtual safety car to be deployed.

Russell took advantage of Perez's misunderstanding of the VSC ending message to secure the final podium slot and join winner Max Verstappen and teammate Lewis Hamilton in the top three.

**LAPS
53**

**CIRCUIT'S
FIRST F1
RACE
1971**

"IS IT OVER?

IT WAS ALL GOING SO WELL FOR CHARLES...

LOVE THE BUCKET HAT

WATER FIGHT!

Matt Gallagher @MattyWTF1
This sport is so heartbreaking sometimes...

"I AM STUPID"

RACE RUNDOWN

POS.	DRIVER
1	VERSTAPPEN
2	HAMILTON
3	RUSSELL
4	PEREZ
5	SAINZ
6	ALONSO
7	NORRIS
8	OCON
9	RICCIARDO
10	STROLL
11	VETTEL
12	GASLY
13	ALBON
14	BOTTAS
15	SCHUMACHER

NON FINISHERS

DNF	ZHOU
DNF	LATIFI
DNF	MAGNUSSEN
DNF	LECLERC
DNF	TSUNODA

FASTEST LAP
1:35.781
SAINZ

TEAM PRINCIPAL

A N A G R A M

Challenge

Can you unscramble the 10 current F1 Team Principals from the names below?

RETURN THIN GEESE	A TITIAN BOTTOM
FONT TZARS	ARSE AND SLIDE
OWL TOT OFF	RACER DRIVES FUSE
SHORT INNER CHAIR	JOTS A TOPIC
AMAZON USER FART	KICK MAKER

65

HUNGARY

"HUGE STRATEGY FAIL"

George Russell lived up to his 'Mr Saturday' nickname in Budapest, securing his first pole position, and come race day kept both Ferraris back until the first round of pitstops.

The overcut benefited Charles Leclerc, who boxed after Carlos Sainz and came out ahead ready to fight Russell for the lead. Soon enough, a stunning overtake around the outside from Charles put him in first place.

All seemed to be going well for Leclerc... *enter the Ferrari strategy team*

Leclerc's second stint on mediums was too short, forcing Ferrari to fit the disastrous hard tyre.

Yep, seriously.

Verstappen, who'd started in tenth after suffering power unit issues in Q3, soon caught up to Charles. Through some fantastic wheel-to-wheel battles, Max passed Leclerc on track before sending himself into a 360° spin, which let Charles through again.

Verstappen soon passed Leclerc on track again for position, with Ferrari eventually bringing him in for soft tyres but this dropped him down to sixth where he'd finish the race.

Lewis Hamilton made some moves on both Carlos Sainz and his teammate Russell to finish second, as Verstappen delivered a stunning drive to win from tenth. A Max title win seemed inevitable as we headed into the summer break...

**LAPS
70**

**CIRCUIT'S FIRST F1 RACE
1986**

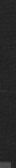

P1 IN FP3: JUST GOATIFI THINGS

FELIZ CUMPLEAÑOS FERNANDO!

'MR SATURDAY' ACTUALLY ON POLE!

POLE TO P3 FOR GEORGE

MAX ADDED 'SPIN AND WIN' TO HIS REPERTOIRE

POS.	DRIVER
1	VERSTAPPEN
2	HAMILTON
3	RUSSELL
4	SAINZ
5	PEREZ
6	LECLERC
7	NORRIS
8	ALONSO
9	OCON
10	VETTEL
11	STROLL
12	GASLY
13	ZHOU
14	SCHUMACHER
15	RICCIARDO
16	MAGNUSSEN
17	ALBON
18	LATIFI
19	TSUNODA

NON FINISHERS
DNF   BOTTAS

68

FASTEST LAP
1:21.386
HAMILTON

wtf1-to-1.

WITH JENSON BUTTON

Who better to review the 2022 F1 season so far than 2009 F1 Champion Jenson Button? We caught up with him to chat about the new regulations, his take on the Verstappen and Leclerc championship battle and who has impressed him in the first half of the season.

What are your thoughts on the new F1 regulations?

I like that we keep having change, I think it's really important. When one team wins all the time it's great for that team, and great for their fans, but at some point they need to throw something in the mix to bring other teams up to their pace.

How have you found the Max and Charles battle this year?

It felt like Charles had the upper hand at the start of the year, he seemed very calm and collected and Max was being quite aggressive. They know each other so well from the karting days, and nothing changes. You see the footage of them both as kids arguing about an 'inchident' and it's no different. They understand each other's driving styles, which I think is important.

Have you been shocked to see so many reliability issues this season?

I'm really surprised. Teams are normally pretty good at realising what's going to happen and stopping the car or changing the engine before the race weekend. With Ferrari, they started the year with such a good car, and they still have a good car, but it's tough for them. This is their best opportunity to win for a few years, and the issues they've got are making it very difficult for themselves.

Who is your driver of the season so far?

If I painted all the cars and crash helmets the same colour, there's one driver that I would always be able to find out of 20, and it's Fernando Alonso. He's got a very different driving style to anyone. He's quite aggressive and the way that he catches slides on exits, he's immediately reacting to it and he's the oldest dude on the grid!

Kevin Magnussen jumping in the car at the first race and doing what he did was exceptional.

It just shows if your head's not in the right place, you don't really do as well as you should. If you come in all excited and the adrenaline's pumping, you can perform.

Do F1 need to ensure historic races are permanently on the calendar?

If Spa isn't there, I'll be very upset.

If you take away Spa, it's for other reasons, and not because it's not a good circuit. It's one of the best in the world. The racing is amazing and drivers love it.*

SCAN TO WATCH THE VIDEO

*GOOD NEWS FOR JB!
SINCE RECORDING THIS INTERVIEW, A ONE-YEAR CONTRACT HAS BEEN SIGNED WHICH MEANS F1 RETURNS TO BELGIUM FOR 2023

69

PIASTRIGATE

How The Piastri Fiasco Unfolded

28.JUL.2022

Seb creates Instagram account to announce retirement

Who replaces Seb?

Codename: The Bee Keeper

SORRY YOU'RE LEAVING

THE FANBOY TIMES
1ST AUGUST 2022

ALONSO TO ASTON MARTIN

Who will take the spare seat at Alpine?

Codename: Le Grand Fromage

otmar's next move?

02.AUG.2022

BWT Alpine F1 Team
@AlpineF1Team

2023 driver line-up confirmed: Esteban Ocon 🔵 Oscar Piastri

After four years as part of the Renault and Alpine family, Reserve Driver Oscar Piastri is promoted to a race seat alongside Esteban Ocon starting from 2023.

EVIDENCE

DRIVER PROFILE

Name
O. PIASTRI
Nationality
AUSTRALIAN
Occupation
RESERVE DRIVER
Likes
SPICY TWEETS
Dislikes
SIMPLE CONTRACT NEGOTIATIONS

O. PIASTRI

Piastri Promoted ✓

BUT LATER THAT DAY...

Oscar Piastri
@OscarPiastri

I understand that, without my agreement, Alpine F1 have put out a press release late this afternoon that I am driving for them next year. This is wrong and I have not signed a contract with Alpine for 2023. I will not be driving for Alpine next year.
:20 · Aug 2, 2022 · Twitter for iPhone

I DON'T ACCESS MY EMAILS **DURING THE RACE**

CONTRACT LAW FOR BEGINNERS   BY SUE U. WALL

Please return to L. Rossi, Alpine

TWEETS

CONTENTS:
100 million
sassy tweets
relating to
#Piastrigate
Written By
LITERALLY EVERYONE

Zak watching
F1 Twitter
explode from
a safe distance

Codename: A River Durchee

Actual Scenes on F1 Twitter

Chaos?
CHAOS.

WTF1 Twitch Stream
WARNING: CONTAINS
SCENES OF SHOEYS
02nd Aussust 2022

Oscar:
"NOPE."

COURT SUMMONS
TO WHOM IT MAY CONCERN:
ALPINE VS McLAREN

Who gets
Piastri?

29th August 2022

What a mess.
I just wanted
to open a
bee hotel!

24.AUG.2022
Honey Badger
announces
McLaren
departure

VERDICT
McLaren's Piastri
Contract Ruled
VALID

CONTRACT RECOGNITION BOARD

02.SEP.2022
Piastri joins
McLaren
for 2023

Where will
Danny Ric
go next?

?

Gasly to Alpine!

BELGIUM

"RED BULL UNTOUCHABLE"

Things got off to a dramatic start at Spa-Francorchamps with old rivals Lewis Hamilton and Fernando Alonso making contact, launching the Mercedes into the air and out of the race. Not one to miss out, Nicholas Latifi spun his Williams a lap later and wiped out Valtteri Bottas in the process.

Championship leader Max Verstappen started the race in 14th, after taking more engine parts, but was on a mission to get another victory. Having set the fastest time in qualifying the day before, it was no secret that Max's car was quick.

Sure enough, it was only a matter of time before Verstappen caught up with pole sitter Carlos Sainz and took the lead with a helping hand from DRS. His teammate Sergio Perez soon did the same and passed Sainz to make it a Red Bull 1-2.

Charles Leclerc, who also served engine penalties in Belgium, managed to recover to fifth towards the end of the race, after an unplanned early pitstop to remove a visor tear-off from his front-right brake duct.

A last-ditch effort for fastest lap didn't pay off either, as he fought Alonso for position before getting a five-second penalty for speeding in the pitlane.

LAPS
44

CIRCUIT'S FIRST F1 RACE
1950

MUST BE LECLERC FANS

THIS IS HOW MUCH DRIVERS LOVE SPA

THAT'S RAIDILLON, ACTUALLY

YEET!

THE W13 MADE A BETTER PORPOISE THAN IT DID A BIRD

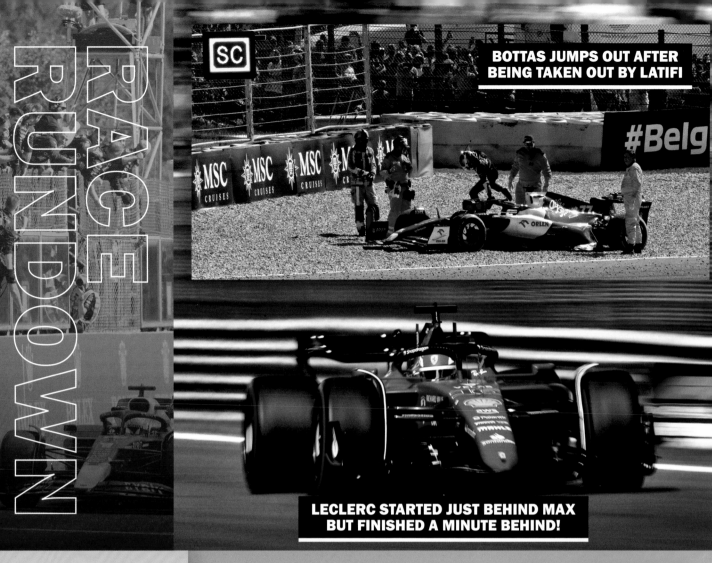

SC

BOTTAS JUMPS OUT AFTER BEING TAKEN OUT BY LATIFI

LECLERC STARTED JUST BEHIND MAX BUT FINISHED A MINUTE BEHIND!

POS.	DRIVER
1	VERSTAPPEN
2	PEREZ
3	SAINZ
4	RUSSELL
5	ALONSO
6	LECLERC
7	OCON
8	VETTEL
9	GASLY
10	ALBON
11	STROLL
12	NORRIS
13	TSUNODA
14	ZHOU
15	RICCIARDO
16	MAGNUSSEN
17	SCHUMACHER
18	LATIFI

NON FINISHERS

DNF	BOTTAS
DNF	HAMILTON

Tom Bellingham @TommyWTF1
That was WILD. Welcome back F1 #BelgianGP

14TH TO 1ST - THIS DAY BELONGED TO VERSTAPPEN

74

FASTEST LAP
1:49.354
VERSTAPPEN

"Dear Katy..."

We all need some good advice every now and again, so who better to help the F1 community than Katy Fairman?

Here are just a few messages that she has received in the last 12 months...

@HungryHungryHorner123

"I have been buying my daily lunches on the company credit card and now we've gone over a strict budget cap.

I feel so guilty, but should I confess it was me?"

Oh dear, love. What a pickle. Sorry, is it too soon for a food pun? Perhaps you should have a quiet word with accounting, and see if they can help on the issue. If it's too late, I would advise holding a press conference about it and finding the best pair of prop glasses you can, to make it look like you mean business. It doesn't matter if nobody has ever seen you with glasses before, just wear them with confidence and people will think you're in an extra serious mode, babes.

@ElPlan1981

"I had this great plan to go back to my old company last year but it wasn't like the old days, so I'm moving jobs again in January. I've met some of the new team, including my new Canadian colleague, but I'm not sure how to take him yet. He just yells 'YOU'RE NOT MY DAD' every time I talk to him.

How can I make the most of my new job?"

Sounds like someone has daddy issues!

Firstly, well done on the new start, sweetie. Changing jobs can be a difficult transition, so just try not to burn any bridges on your way out (you've already returned to that company before, so you never know if you'll be back again).

Different things motivate us at different stages of life; success, a big wodge of cash, a sweet company car... so just think about what you want out of this next chapter and give it everything you have.

Regarding your new Canadian colleague, a wise man once said to me "all the time, you have to leave the space".

So just do that and I'm sure you'll be fine.

@TrafficParadise

"What's the best cure for heartbreak? My best friend at work is moving to a rival company and although I feel upset and betrayed, I still love him and will miss his presence in the team.

How do I cope without my bestie?"

There's nothing worse than the pain of losing that first love, so I feel for you hun. I'd always recommend some good food, wine and a rom-com to get over the initial pain, but remember this isn't the end, it could just be the beginning.

Perhaps you'll find that the relationship was holding you back; now you can now spread your wings and become the leader those around you need. And if all else fails, you can leave the company and go do something completely different, maybe set up your own restaurant?

NETHERLANDS

"NO STOPPING VERSTAPPEN"

Max Verstappen wanted to give the Orange Army a treat as sweet as stroopwafels by getting his fourth win in a row. After securing pole position and leading the opening stages everything seemed to be under control, but the same couldn't be said for Ferrari.

Carlos Sainz was the victim of a missing left-rear tyre during his first stop, with the situation going from bad to worse when Sergio Perez ran over the abandoned wheel gun belonging to the Scuderia.

Later in the race, Yuki Tsunoda pulled over complaining his tyres hadn't been fitted properly during his recent stop. AlphaTauri assured him all was fine, but pitted him again as a precaution. The car still wasn't fixed, so Yuki parked at the side of the track, causing a virtual safety car just as Mercedes seemed to be in striking distance of Max's Red Bull. This sent F1's conspiracy theorists wild!

A late safety car (after Valtteri Bottas broke down) bunched the field, with Lewis Hamilton now leading but a sitting duck on worn tyres as the others pitted.

Once racing resumed, Max shot past Lewis to take the lead with George Russell almost going up the back of Hamilton to pass him for second. Leclerc did the same, getting that final podium spot.

LAPS
72

CIRCUIT'S FIRST F1 RACE
1952

MAX GETTING A LIFT FROM DUTCH KICKBOXER RICO VERHOEVEN

"THEN HE JUST PICKED ME UP..."

TSUNODA BREAKS THE INTERNET WITH F1 CONSPIRACY THEORIES

Tom Bellingham @TommyWTF1
Ferrari, F1 cars have four tyres
#DutchGP

RACE RUNDOWN

THE T3 BANKING CREATED SOME GREAT SIDE BY SIDE RACING

POS.	DRIVER
1	VERSTAPPEN
2	RUSSELL
3	LECLERC
4	HAMILTON
5	PEREZ
6	ALONSO
7	NORRIS
8	SAINZ
9	OCON
10	STROLL
11	GASLY
12	ALBON
13	SCHUMACHER
14	VETTEL
15	MAGNUSSEN
16	ZHOU
17	RICCIARDO
18	LATIFI

NON FINISHERS

DNF	BOTTAS
DNF	TSUNODA

FASTEST LAP
1:13.652
VERSTAPPEN

Ferrari's WHEEL OF MISFORTUNE!

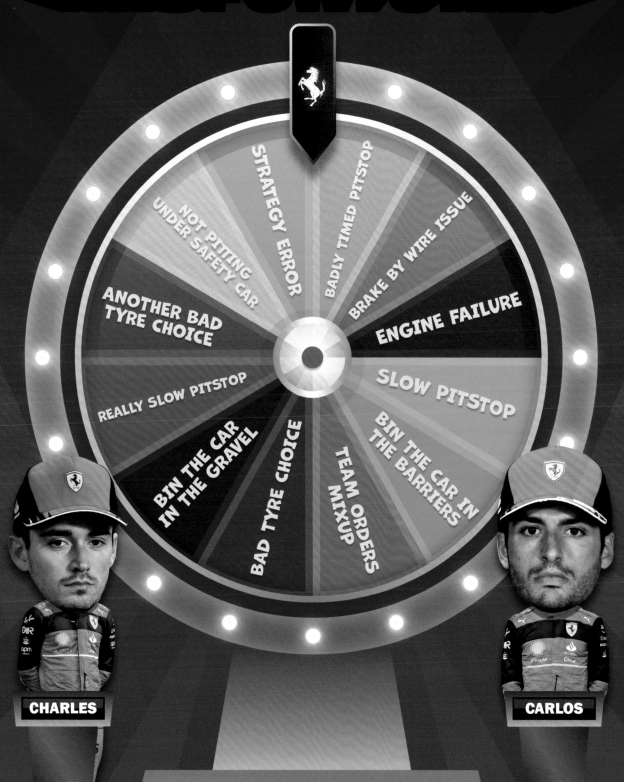

There seemed to be times this year when Ferrari's race strategy was decided more by the spin of a wheel than it was by analysis and insight - so step right up and put it to the test and spin, spin, spin the wheel of Ferrari (mis)fortune!

ITALY

The Tifosi went wild as polesitter Charles Leclerc led the grid away at Monza, but an unlucky strategy call soon unravelled Leclerc's race. Ferrari gambled on pitting Leclerc during an early virtual safety car for Sebastian Vettel's broken down Aston Martin, but racing resumed just as Leclerc left his pit box.

Things were made worse as Charles' championship rival Max Verstappen, who had started seventh with engine penalties, had made his way up to second in just five laps and now inherited the lead.

Both drivers ahead of Leclerc - Verstappen and George Russell - made their soft tyres last twice as long with Leclerc forced into a two-stop strategy with everyone around him on a one-stop. Verstappen maintained the lead with Charles slowly closing the gap on soft tyres in the final stages of the race.

However, just five laps from the chequered flag Daniel Ricciardo's McLaren broke down, causing a safety car. The top four all peeled into the pits for a fresh set of tyres, but with the McLaren stuck in gear and no easy way of removing it, the race ended under safety car conditions.

No overtaking at the end of the race meant Nyck de Vries scored two points on his F1 debut after Alex Albon was struck down with appendicitis on qualifying day.

"UNLUCKY FERRARI STRATEGY"

LAPS
53

CIRCUIT'S FIRST F1 RACE
1950

AUTODROMO NAZIONALE MONZA
09 - 11 SEP 2022

IS THAT A MINION?
OH! NO, IT'S
CHARLES LECLERC!

NOT FLUORESCENT AERO PAINT,
JUST FERRARI'S BIRTHDAY LIVERY

NYCK, DUDE, SHOULDN'T
YOU BE OVER THERE?

WHO ELSE?!

WHEN UNRELIABILITY THWARTS
EL PLAN - BUT YOU STILL LOVE IT

RACE RUNDOWN

ALWAYS A DRAMATIC START IN MAGIC MONZA

POS.	DRIVER
1	VERSTAPPEN
2	LECLERC
3	RUSSELL
4	SAINZ
5	HAMILTON
6	PEREZ
7	NORRIS
8	GASLY
9	DE VRIES
10	ZHOU
11	OCON
12	SCHUMACHER
13	BOTTAS
14	TSUNODA
15	LATIFI
16	MAGNUSSEN

NON FINISHERS

DNF	RICCIARDO
DNF	STROLL
DNF	ALONSO
DNF	VETTEL

Matt Gallagher @MattyWTF1
Petition for De Vries to do the rest of the season alongside Albon #ItalianGP #F1

82

FASTEST LAP
1:24.030
PEREZ

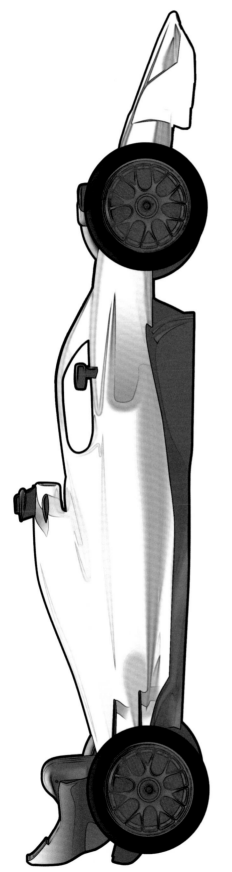

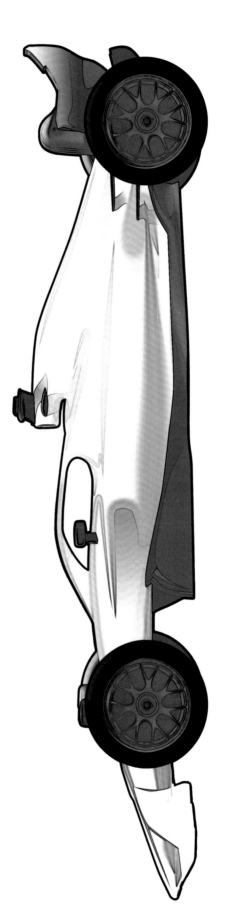

Tommy's Livery Design Challenge

We've seen some awesome one-off liveries this year,
but do you think you could do any better?

Share your final designs with us using the hashtag #WTF1Annual

After a pre-race downpour delayed lights out, Sergio Perez wasted no time passing Charles Leclerc for the lead of the race. Aside from Alex Albon's little spin, the field navigated the wet track well until Nicholas Latifi wiped out Zhou Guanyu and caused a safety car.

Max Verstappen arrived in Singapore with a mathematical chance of winning the title. However, his race got off to a bad start, having started from eighth, and he fell back to 13th. Despite making up places, a dramatic lock-up when fighting Lando Norris send Max shooting down an escape road. He stopped for new tyres and recovered again from almost last.

Drivers up and down the grid made mistakes too, with Lewis Hamilton making contact with a barrier half way into the race when hunting down Carlos Sainz. Laps later, Yuki Tsunoda brought out a full safety car when he ploughed into the tecpro. George Russell also made contact with Mick Schumacher, after the Mercedes driver started from the pitlane.

Both Alpine drivers also had a nightmare race, as Fernando Alonso retired with engine issues on his record-breaking 350th start while Esteban Ocon was forced to get the subway back to the garage after his power unit went bang.

Sergio kept his cool in the Singapore heat, winning again at another street circuit.

LAPS
59

CIRCUIT'S
FIRST F1
RACE
2008

"CRAZY WEATHER CONDITIONS"

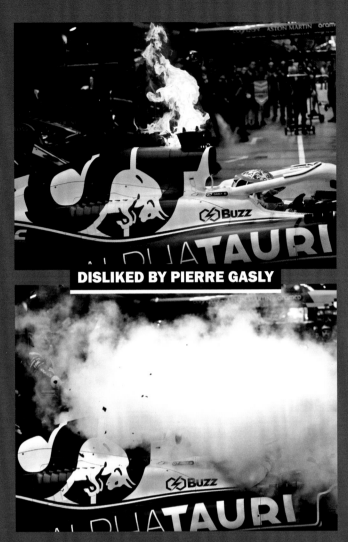

DISLIKED BY PIERRE GASLY

**WHEN IT'S WET OUTSIDE
BUT YOU WANT TO GO OUT
AND PLAY WITH YOUR MATES**

MARINA BAE

SCREW THE SAFETY CAR, I'LL GO AT MY OWN PACE!

POS.	DRIVER
1	PEREZ
2	LECLERC
3	SAINZ
4	NORRIS
5	RICCIARDO
6	STROLL
7	VERSTAPPEN
8	VETTEL
9	HAMILTON
10	GASLY
11	BOTTAS
12	MAGNUSSEN
13	SCHUMACHER

NON FINISHERS

DNF	RUSSELL
DNF	TSUNODA
DNF	OCON
DNF	ALBON
DNF	ALONSO
DNF	LATIFI
DNF	ZHOU

LECLERC HAD POLE BUT FLUFFED THE START

WTF1 @wtf1official
Albon is going to retire from the race, but what an effort from him this weekend after his recent surgery 👏 #SingaporeGP

FASTEST LAP
1:46.458
RUSSELL

F101

STAY COOL BABY

The Singapore Grand Prix is one of the hottest races on the F1 calendar. It's crazy humid and makes the already demanding job of driving an F1 car even harder. There are steps the drivers can take though to help keep them cool. Some happen in the car, others are preparation that takes place weeks or months beforehand.

Let's start with the prep work.

For some drivers, acclimatising and adjusting themselves to the temperatures is the first step. Exercising with race suits on to replicate the conditions can help, with the more training to prepare for the heat and humidity, the better. Heat should become second nature to a driver, so all their focus can be on the challenge of racing and not thinking about the weather every few seconds.

Over the actual weekend, drivers can treat themselves to a cheeky ICE BATH which helps reduce your body temperature. It's also understood that ice baths have other benefits like speeding up recovery time and reducing inflammation of muscle tissue.

Now onto the clothing.

All the clothing that the drivers wear has to meet very strict safety standards. The race suit consists of three layers, and with additional underwear and balaclavas, as well as gloves and boots, you can see why they are dripping in sweat after a long day in the car. It's exhausting work.

Thanks to modern technology, these garments are made from lightweight and breathable materials. These make it more comfortable for the driver and also help combat heat stress.

For underwear, there are also fabrics that help move a driver's sweat to the top layer of the material - and are quick-drying so the drivers are not sat in a pool of their own sweat for hours.

Before the start of a race, you might also see drivers opting for a snazzy COOLING VEST or a good ol' wet towel around the neck. The cooling vests come with pouches filled with ice packs and are a common sight on the grid.

Drinking is also vital in these temperatures and drivers are allowed to fill up their bottles with 1.5 LITRES of drinking fluid before a race - we'd totally recommend an ice slushy during these hot races but we're not sure if that's allowed.

It's estimated that a driver can lose around 3KG of their weight just from sweating alone during the Singapore Grand Prix!

JAPAN

"TWO TIME CHAMPION"

With very wet starting conditions and all the grid on intermediate tyres, it didn't take long for the Japanese Grand Prix to be red flagged following a big crash for Carlos Sainz.

The Ferrari driver aquaplained into a barrier, with Pierre Gasly picking up an advertising board that came loose. Replays also showed Gasly coming extremely close to a recovery vehicle on track during the red flag, with drivers understandably furious at the situation.

Two hours later, racing resumed with a rolling start and mandatory full wet tyres. Nicholas Latifi and Sebastian Vettel instantly came into the pits for the inters, and were soon flying with other drivers then copying the switch over. Mick Schumacher stayed out as the only driver on the wet tyre, and led the race for a split second, before tumbling down the pack and eventually finishing last.

Despite Esteban Ocon 'defending like a lion' from Lewis Hamilton for fourth, all eyes were on the battle for second. Sergio Perez had closed the gap to Charles Leclerc, but a last corner mistake from Charles made him bypass the chicane to stay ahead!

Max Verstappen crossed the finish line in first, and after clarification on the championship points on offer for the race distance completed and a post-race penalty for Leclerc, Verstappen was crowned the 2022 F1 world champion in parc ferme!

JAPANESE F1 FANS

NEVER DISAPPOINT

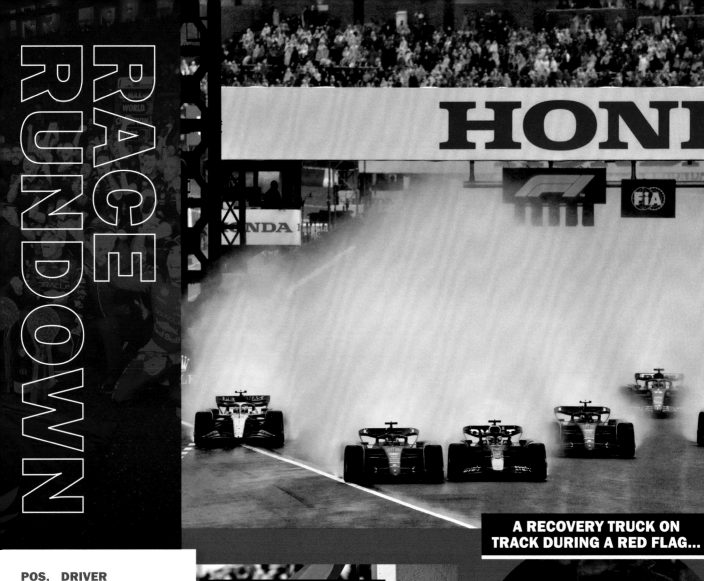

RACE RUNDOWN

POS.	DRIVER
1	VERSTAPPEN
2	PEREZ
3	LECLERC
4	OCON
5	HAMILTON
6	VETTEL
7	ALONSO
8	RUSSELL
9	LATIFI
10	NORRIS
11	RICCIARDO
12	STROLL
13	TSUNODA
14	MAGNUSSEN
15	BOTTAS
16	ZHOU
17	SCHUMACHER
18	GASLY

NON FINISHERS

DNF	SAINZ
DNF	ALBON

A RECOVERY TRUCK ON TRACK DURING A RED FLAG...

SAINZ CRASH BRINGS OUT THE RED FLAG

...MADE GASLY FURIOUS WITH RACE CONTROL

90

FASTEST LAP
1:44.411
ZHOU

TWO-TIME CHAMP CLUB SELFIE!

USA

Carlos Sainz qualified fastest for the second time this season, but his race was over at Turn 1 after being punted by George Russsell who got a five-second penalty for the offence.

Valtteri Bottas also had a nightmare, as small contact with Sergio Perez on the first lap was later followed by being beached in the gravel. The incident required a safety car, but once it had ended it was quickly deployed again for another accident.

Future teammates, Fernando Alonso and Lance Stroll, came together which resulted in Alonso's car being sent airbourne.

Stroll was at fault and out of the race, but Fernando could miraculously continue in his very beaten up Alpine. Both drivers were thankfully ok.

Later in the race, Charles Leclerc sent it past Sergio Perez for the final podium spot, as Lewis Hamilton chased down race leader Max Verstappen.

Max experienced a rare slow pitstop and was forced to come out behind Leclerc and fight for position on track - it had been a while since we saw these two going wheel-to-wheel! Verstappen overtook Hamilton with six laps to go to secure another race win.

Sebastian Vettel, who also led the race at one point, had an epic final lap and stunned us all with a truly awesome overtake on Kevin Magnussen for eighth.

**LAPS
56**

**CIRCUIT'S
FIRST F1
RACE
2012**

" **STILL GOT IT** "

WHERE ELSE WOULD YOU FIND A VIP HORSE?

GETTING INTO THE SPIRIT OF TEXAS

RUSSELL SENDS SAINZ INTO A SPIN AT THE FIRST CORNER!

RACE RUNDOWN

STROLL GETS A PENALTY FOR CAUSING A COLLISION WITH FERNANDO...

...AND ALONSO STILL FINISHED 7TH!

SEB STORMS TO 8TH!

SHAQ'S BACK!

MAX WINS TO SECURE RED BULL'S TITLE DOUBLE!

Katy Fairman @katyfairman
Red Bull win the 2022 F1 Constructors' Championship, ending eight years of Mercedes dominance. The team last won the title in 2013, and dedicated the win to their owner Dietrich Mateschitz who passed away the day before. #USGP

POS.	DRIVER
1	VERSTAPPEN
2	HAMILTON
3	LECLERC
4	PEREZ
5	RUSSELL
6	NORRIS
7	ALONSO
8	VETTEL
9	MAGNUSSEN
10	TSUNODA
11	OCON
12	ZHOU
13	ALBON
14	GASLY
15	SCHUMACHER
16	RICCIARDO
17	LATIFI

NON FINISHERS

DNF	STROLL
DNF	BOTTAS
DNF	SAINZ

94

FASTEST LAP
1:38.788
RUSSELL

WE WANT YOUR HOT TAKES

LANDO *will never win a* **WDC** *if he doesn't leave* **McLAREN**

MILD
Colder than winter testing

The **WORST PERFORMING** *driver on points at the end of each season should be* **REMOVED** *to make way for another* **NEW DRIVER**

MEDIUM
Tongue like a tyre blanket

LECLERC *will join* **MERCEDES** *when* **HAMILTON** *retires*

HOT HOT HOT
Flaming disc brakes!

DO YOU HAVE A HOT TAKE?

JOIN WTF1 LIVE ON TWITCH FOR
HOT TAKES WEDNESDAY
WHERE WE SHARE AND RATE
THE HEAT OF YOUR SPICY TAKES
ON THE LATEST GOINGS ON
IN THE WORLD OF F1.

TWITCH.COM/WTF1OFFICIAL

TEAM WTF1 *Global* FAN GALLERY

Friends Soléne & Maartje check out the Belgium GP together for the first time

Matt & Sarah visit Monza, the Temple of Speed

It's not just the teams that travel the world for Formula One.

Here is a selection of globe-trotting TEAM WTF1 members who were lucky enough to see live F1 racing this year.

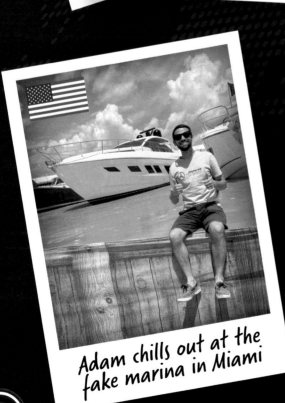

Adam chills out at the fake marina in Miami

Craig, Sam and Lawrence making new friends at the Dutch GP

Heni in Hungary

Jonathan & Kai dodging
the rain in Singapore

Wish you were here!

PIEEEEEERRE GASSSLLYYY

Anna & Tom take Miami

K-MAG!

"RECORDS ARE BROKEN"

**LAPS
71**

**CIRCUIT'S
FIRST F1
RACE
1963**

As the grid slipstreamed their way down to Turn 1, Max Verstappen kept the lead as both Mercedes drivers got their elbows out behind him.

Lewis Hamilton overtook George Russell for second before chasing after Max's Red Bull, while Sergio Perez took advantage of Hamilton forcing Russell wide at Turn 3 to grab third - much to the enjoyment of the crowd.

With Verstappen starting on the softs and Hamilton on the mediums, a strategy battle for the win commenced. Lewis inherited the lead on lap 25 as Verstappen made the switch to mediums, with Hamilton moving to the hard compound later on before stating the "tyre isn't good".

Elsewhere on track, Daniel Ricciardo collided with Yuki Tsunoda in the battle for 11th and took the AlphaTauri driver out of the race for which he was given a 10-second penalty. However, this sanction lit a fire inside of the Honey Badger who flew through the field on soft tyres to finish best of the rest, even with the added penalty time.

In the end, Verstappen nursed his medium tyres until the chequered flag and earned his 14th win of the season - a new F1 record.

His teammate Perez kept the home crowd happy by finishing on the incredible Mexican podium finishing third - not far behind Hamilton's Mercedes.

AUTÓDROMO HERMANOS RODRÍGUEZ
28 - 30 OCT 2022

URBAN ARTIST FERMÍN LA CALACA CREATES CUSTOM JACKET FOR ALONSO

SO MUCH LOVE FOR CHECO

PEREZ MAKING MOVES ON THE FIRST LAP

RACE RUNDOWN

YET MORE MECHANICAL WOES FOR FERNANDO

POS.	DRIVER
1	VERSTAPPEN
2	HAMILTON
3	PEREZ
4	RUSSELL
5	SAINZ
6	LECLERC
7	RICCIARDO
8	OCON
9	NORRIS
10	BOTTAS
11	GASLY
12	ALBON
13	ZHOU
14	VETTEL
15	STROLL
16	SCHUMACHER
17	MAGNUSSEN
18	LATIFI

NON FINISHERS

DNF	ALONSO
DNF	TSUNODA

WTF1 @wtf1official
Verstappen now breaks the record for the most wins EVER in a season of F1 🏆🏆🏆🏆🏆🏆🏆🏆🏆🏆🏆🏆🏆🏆
#MexicoGP

FASTEST LAP
1:20.153
RUSSELL

Since making his F1 debut in 2007 with BMW Sauber, four-time champion Sebastian Vettel became one of the most beloved characters in the paddock. His retirement at the end of this season is the end of an era, so Tommy, Matt and Katy decided to reflect on three key chapters of Seb's career.

SEB'S LEG...

TOMMY ON RED BULL

2009 - 2013

Vettel and Red Bull are one of those iconic duos in F1.

It took Seb just his third race with the team to get Red Bull Racing their first victory and his second season with them to secure their first world titles. At times the combination of Sebastian Vettel and Red Bull looked absolutely unbeatable, with no better example of this being the record-breaking nine consecutive wins at the end of a dominant 2013 season, an F1 record not even the likes of Michael Schumacher and Lewis Hamilton could achieve during their most successful years. After four world titles in a row, Seb struggled in the first year of the new turbo hybrid era, a year that turned out to be his last with Red Bull as the German wanted to continue his legacy at the legendary Ferrari in the hope of emulating his hero, Michael Schumacher.

MATT ON FERRARI

2015 - 2020

At times, this was a beautiful combination.

Vettel won 14 races for Ferrari, and fought for the title in 2017 and 2018, but it just didn't work out the way everyone thought it would. There were some amazing team radio moments over the years of him singing after winning or claiming there was 'something loose between his legs', typical Seb banter.

You could really tell it meant the world to him to drive for Ferrari with how much he loves F1 history. However, it ended pretty sourly with Ferrari not offering him a contract extension after 2020 and instead going for Carlos Sainz which shocked a lot of people. Charles Leclerc was the new Ferrari focus in town and Seb had to search for a seat elsewhere.

KATY ON ASTON MARTIN

2021 - 2022

The final chapter, for now.

Although his results on paper weren't the best, Sebastian's time at Aston Martin showed fans a side to him we'd never fully seen before. Across his final few years in F1, Seb used his platform to bring attention to environmental and social causes that he cared about, from rising sea levels in Miami and saving the bees, to proudly displaying support to the LGBTQA+ community with his "Same Love" message.

Of course, he helped bring success to Aston Martin's return too, with two podiums during the 2021 season in Baku and Hungary (although the latter was disqualified due to a lack of fuel sample). However, I think most of us will remember these two years as the time he secured a place in our hearts, never to leave it.

"NON-STOP ACTION"

LAPS
71

CIRCUIT'S FIRST F1 RACE
1973

You know you're in for a wild weekend when Kevin Magnussen is on pole.

That was the reality at Interlagos when George Russell beached his Mercedes in Q3, rain started to fall, and Magnussen was fastest on the slick tyres. Nobody could beat his time due to the conditions, Haas got their first pole position and it was SO DAMN WHOLESOME!

Then came the Sprint. Max Verstappen soon passed Kevin for the lead, with K-Mag eventually falling down to eighth. Both Alpine drivers broke the first rule of racing - don't hit your teammate - and came together twice, finishing the event near the back. Lance Stroll also missed the memo, pushing Sebastian Vettel off the track and earning a 10-second penalty.

Russell fought Verstappen for first over several epic laps, with George emerging on top. Carlos Sainz then made contact with Max when fighting for position, leaving the

Red Bull car wounded and allowing Lewis Hamilton to get up to third.

Race day kicked off with a Mercedes 1-2 as Sainz took an engine penalty, with Russell getting a perfect start on the hunt for his first win. A safety car was deployed for a first-lap collision between Daniel Ricciardo and Magnussen, and once racing resumed old rivals Verstappen and Hamilton clashed with Max deemed to be at fault. Lando Norris then tapped Charles Leclerc and sent him into the wall, *all in one lap!*

During the final stages, Sergio Perez struggled on the medium tyre but allowed Verstappen past to attack both Ferraris on one condition; he'd give Perez the place back if he failed. However, when given team orders on the final lap to let Checo through, Max refused!

The Red Bull drama overshadowed Russell's maiden win, and Mercedes' first victory since the 2021 Saudi Arabian Grand Prix.

"ER, GUYS. WHY IS EVERYONE ELSE ON SLICKS?"

LOOKING LIKE A BUNCH OF 'LEGENDS'

K-MAG ABSOLUTELY FOK-SMASHED IT

K-MAG LEADS THE PACK AT THE START OF THE SPRINT

FOOD POISONING, PENALTIES AND AN ENGINE FAILURE MADE IT A BIRTHDAY WEEKEND TO FORGET FOR NORRIS

GEORGE KEEPS A COOL HEAD WHILST THE DRAMA UNFOLDS

POS.	DRIVER
1	RUSSELL
2	HAMILTON
3	SAINZ
4	LECLERC
5	ALONSO
6	VERSTAPPEN
7	PEREZ
8	OCON
9	BOTTAS
10	STROLL
11	VETTEL
12	ZHOU
13	SCHUMACHER
14	GASLY
15	ALBON
16	LATIFI
17	TSUNODA

NON FINISHERS

DNF	NORRIS
DNF	MAGNUSSEN
DNF	RICCIARDO

LECLERC SURVIVES A BRUSH WITH THE WALL TO TAKE FOURTH

104

FASTEST LAP
1:13.785
RUSSELL

'YEAH, ABOUT THAT CRASH IN MONACO...'

Katy Fairman @katyfairman
I'm sorry but if I was Perez and heard that radio from Max flat out denying to let me through I'd be seething. Think of all the times he's helped him out and kept drivers behind to benefit Max. Not impressed... #BrazilGP

FIRST-TIME WINNER

GEEEOOORRRGE!

MR SATURDAY BECOMES MR SUNDAY

ABU DHABI

"ALL THE EMOTION"

LAPS
58

**CIRCUIT'S
FIRST F1
RACE
2009**

Red Bull managed their only front-row lock out of the season, as Max Verstappen got ready to convert pole into his 15th win of 2022.

Lewis Hamilton and Carlos Sainz came close to contact fighting for fourth which resulted in Hamilton running wide and over a kerb on the first lap, later having to give the position back to Sainz. The two continued back and forth, until Hamilton reported a loss of power and teammate George Russell swept through.

El Plan took one final hit as halfway through Fernando Alonso's final race with Alpine, he retired with a water leak.

Nicholas Latifi and Mick Schumacher, two drivers out of contract for next season, found themselves in a synchronised spin with Mick getting a penalty for the incident.

Elsewhere Ferrari perfected their final race strategy - *yes really* - keeping Charles Leclerc on a one-stop whilst Red Bull pitted Sergio Perez twice. With these two equal on points, and second place in the drivers' championship up for grabs, whoever finished ahead would become 'vice champion'. Checo fought his way through the field, but couldn't reach Leclerc and finished third.

Vettel was dealt an awful strategy for his final F1 race, but still managed to secure a championship point after Hamilton retired with a hydraulic issue. We even got treated to some final celebratory donuts from the four-time champ!

RED BULL FINALLY GET THEIR FIRST FRONT ROW LOCKOUT OF THE YEAR

Tom Bellingham @TommyWTF1
Hamilton putting Vettel in the points. Respect 👏😄 #AbuDhabiGP

RUSSELL AND NORRIS ALMOST COLLIDE IN THE PITLANE

THE FIA MADE A SPECIAL ALLOWANCE FOR SEB TO DO DONUTS AT THE END OF HIS FINAL F1 RACE

POS.	DRIVER
1	VERSTAPPEN
2	LECLERC
3	PEREZ
4	SAINZ
5	RUSSELL
6	NORRIS
7	OCON
8	STROLL
9	RICCIARDO
10	VETTEL
11	TSUNODA
12	ZHOU
13	ALBON
14	GASLY
15	BOTTAS
16	SCHUMACHER
17	MAGNUSSEN

NON FINISHERS

DNF	HAMILTON
DNF	LATIFI
DNF	ALONSO

LADIES AND GENTLEMEN, THE CLASS OF 2022

108

FASTEST LAP
1:28.391
NORRIS

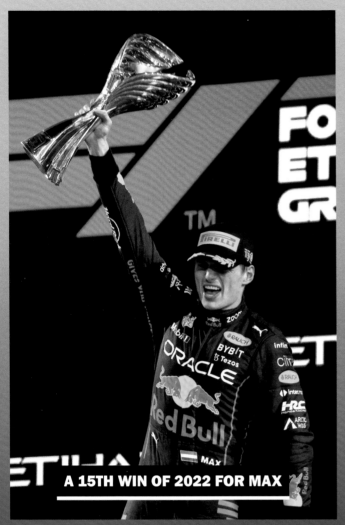

A 15TH WIN OF 2022 FOR MAX

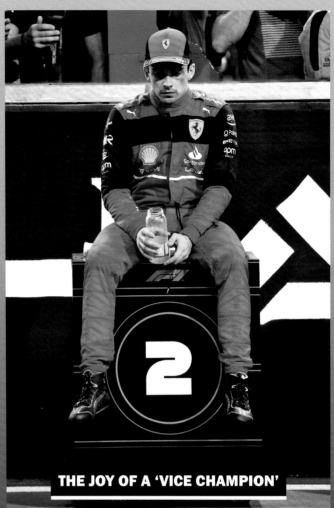

THE JOY OF A 'VICE CHAMPION'

"WAIT, THE SEASON IS OVER ALREADY?!"

2022 F1 DRIVERS' CHAMPIONSHIP STANDINGS

POS.		DRIVER	TEAM	POINTS
01		Max Verstappen	Red Bull	454
02		Charles Leclerc	Ferrari	308
03		Sergio Perez	Red Bull	305
04		George Russell	Mercedes	275
05		Carlos Sainz	Ferrari	246
06		Lewis Hamilton	Mercedes	240
07		Lando Norris	McLaren	122
08		Esteban Ocon	Alpine	92
09		Fernando Alonso	Alpine	81
10		Valtteri Bottas	Alfa Romeo	49
11		Daniel Ricciardo	McLaren	37
12		Sebastian Vettel	Aston Martin	37
13		Kevin Magnussen	Haas	25
14		Pierre Gasly	AlphaTauri	23
15		Lance Stroll	Aston Martin	18
16		Mick Schumacher	Haas	12
17		Yuki Tsunoda	AlphaTauri	12
18		Zhou Guanyu	Alfa Romeo	6
19		Alexander Albon	Williams	4
20		Nicholas Latifi	Williams	2
21		Nyck De Vries	Williams	2
22		Nico Hülkenberg	Aston Martin	0

TWO-TIME WORLD CHAMPION

GRAND PRIX WINS	15
POLE POSITIONS	7
SPRINT RACE WINS	2
OTHER PODIUMS	2
POINTS	454

POS.	TEAM	POINTS
01	Red Bull	759
02	Ferrari	554
03	Mercedes	515
04	Alpine	173
05	McLaren	159
06	Alfa Romeo	55
07	Aston Martin	55
08	Haas	37
09	AlphaTauri	35
10	Williams	8

FIVE-TIME CONSTRUCTORS' CHAMPIONS

RED BULL

2010 — 2011 — 2012 — 2013 — 2022

ABCDEF1 — 2022 REPORT CARD

ROUND	1 Max Verstappen	11 Sergio Perez	55 Carlos Sainz	16 Charles Leclerc	63 George Russell	44 Lewis Hamilton	31 Esteban Ocon	14 Fernando Alonso	3 Daniel Ricciardo	4 Lando Norris	77 Valtteri Bottas	24 Zhou Guanyu	18 Lance Stroll	5 Sebastian Vettel	27 Nico Hülkenberg	20 Kevin Magnussen	47 Mick Schumacher	10 Pierre Gasly	22 Yuki Tsunoda	23 Alexander Albon	6 Nicholas Latifi	45 Nyck de Vries
01	A	B	A	A*	B	A	B	C	D	C	A	A	C	-	C	A*	B	B	B	B	E	-
02	A	A*	B	A	B	D	B	A	B	B	B	C	D	-	C	B	E	B	DNS	D	F	-
03	A	A	D	A*	A	A	B	C	A	A	B	C	E	E		D	D	C	D	A*	E	-
04	A*	A	C	C	A	D	D	C	D	A*	A*	D	B	A		B	E	D	A	B	D	-
05	A*	B	B	B	A	B	B	A	D	C	C	A	C	B		C	D	C	D	A	D	-
06	A	A	C	A*	A	A*	A	A	A	D	A	C	D	C		D	C	D	B	D	C	-
07	B	A*	A*	A*	A	C	C	B	D	A	B	D	E	B		C	E	A	D	D	F	-
08	A	A	B	A	A	C	B	B	B	C	A	D	A*	B		B	E	A*	A	D	E	-
09	A*	D	A	B	B	A	B	A	C	C	B	A	B	C		D	B	C	D	C	C	-
10	A	A	A	A	C	A	C	A	E	A	C	A	C	A		B	A	C	E	C	B	-
11	A	C	A	A*	B	A	A*	A	B	B	B	C	C	C		A	A*	E	D	B	D	-
12	A*	C	C	A*	F	A	A*	C	A	B	B	D	E	B		C	D	C	B	C	D	-
13	A*	C	B	B	A*	B	B	D	B	C	C	C	B	C		D	C	E	C	C	C	-
14	A*	A	A	B	A	E	A*	A	C	C	C	C	C	A		C	C	A*	C	A*	F	-
15	A*	C	C	A	A	A	B	A*	E	A	C	C	B	D		E	B	C	B	B	F	-
16	A*	C	A	A	A	A	D	C	C	B	C	B	D	D		E	C	A	C	-	F	A*
17	D	A*	C	A	E	D	C	A	A	A*	C	D	A*	A		D	D	B	E	E	F	-
18	A*	A	E	B	B	B	A*	B	C	C	D	D	C	A		C	D	D	C	D	A*	-
19	A*	B	B	B	A	C	A*	C	F	A*	D	C	F	A*		A	D	C	B	B	E	-
20	A*	A	B	C	B	A	B	B	A	B	B	C	C	C		D	D	D	B	B	F	-
21	C	B	A	B	A*	A	B	A	F	C	B	C	C	B		A	C	D	E	C	F	-
22	A*	B	B	A*	B	B	A	B	B	A	D	C	A	A		D	D	D	B	B	E	-
AVERAGE	A	B	B	A	B	B	B	B	C	B	B	C	C	B	C	B	C	C	C	C	E	A*

114

SO, FINAL THOUGHTS?

MATT

The 2022 season was certainly different to 2021, wasn't it? A lot more of a 'normal' season I suppose you could call it, with a runaway title winner and Ferrari just... doing Ferrari things.

It's been an amazing year as always at WTF1 though, being able to connect with so many of you through our race watchalongs, on social media or meeting a lot of you at race tracks or even my local shops!! It means the world to continue doing this, having made a huge F1 family that we can all share our terrible opinions with. As the 2022 season closes and we look ahead to 2023, I really hope I can get the 'Ferrari Hype Train' hoodie back out and be a deluded Ferrari fan once more at the start of next year. See you there!

When Max Verstappen was sat 46 points behind in the championship after two failures in three races, I did not expect to be writing about a dominant Verstappen title victory – but that's the power of the Grace onesie for you! While the title fight might not have been anywhere near as spicy as last year, we've still had a hugely enjoyable year.

Be it race watchalongs, our podcast or streaming on Twitch during some crazy silly season announcements, it's been great making the WTF1 motto of 'by fans for fans' ring truer than ever. Thank you as always for the love and support we get from this community and you'll be pleased to know that the Max onesie has been retired so we should get a much closer and more exciting season in 2023!

TOMMY

KATY

Here we are. The end of ANOTHER awesome F1 season, and what a year it's been. New regulations shook up the order, silly season reached new levels of chaos and we even celebrated two new winners in Carlos Sainz and George Russell. Well done, lads. We also said emotional goodbyes to some of our favourite drivers, although let's hope it's more of a 'see ya later'.

But of course, we wouldn't be here writing this annual, recording the podcast, hosting Clubhouse, or goofing about on watchalongs without all of you and your incredible support.

You really are the absolute best.

ANSWERS

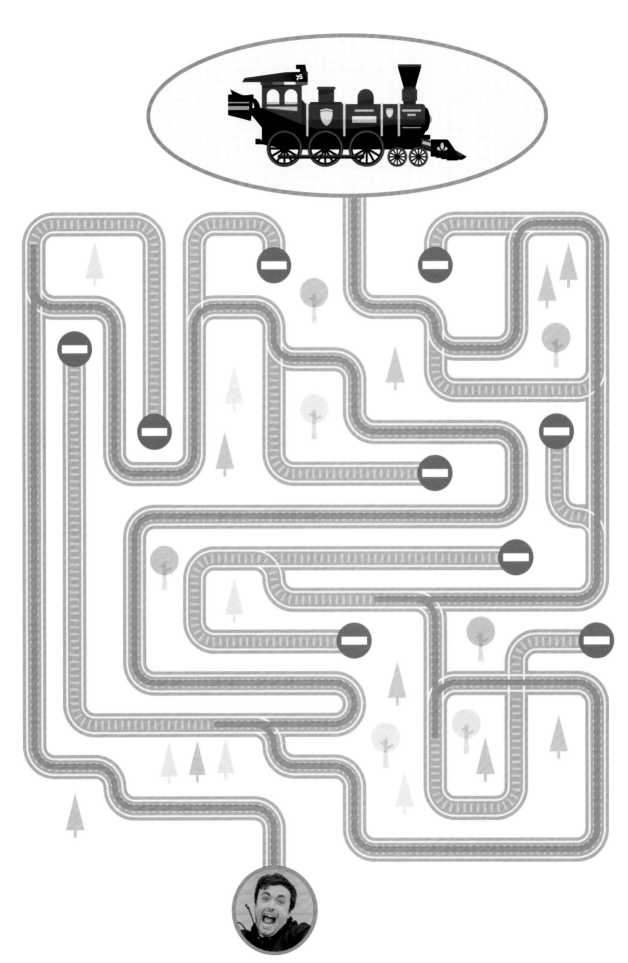

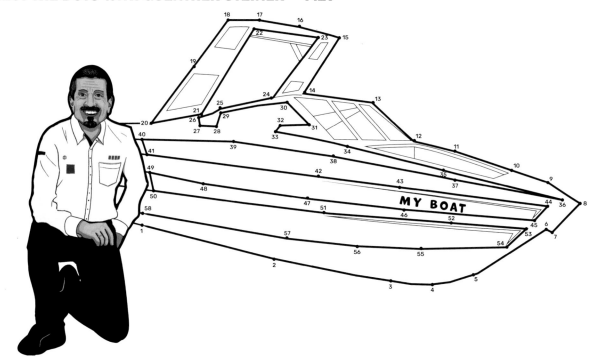

MY BOAT

GUESS THE RACE TRACK   P.49

Circuit of the Americas
USA

Autodromo Nazionale Monza
Italy

Circuit Paul Ricard
France

Red Bull Ring
Austria

Bahrain International Circuit
Bahrain

Silverstone Circuit
UK

Miami International Autodrome
USA

Circuit Gilles Villeneuve
Canada

TEAM PRINCIPAL   P.65
ANAGRAM CHALLENGE

Return Thin Geese
Guenther Steiner

Font Tzars
Franz Tost

Owl Tot Off
Toto Wolff

Short Inner Chair
Christian Horner

Amazon User Fart
Otmar Szafnauer

A Titian Bottom
Mattia Binotto

Arse and Slide
Andreas Seidl

Racer Drives Fuse
Frédéric Vasseur

Jots A Topic
Jost Capito

Kick Maker
Mike Krack

ACKNOWLEDGEMENTS

WE WOULD LIKE TO THANK THE FOLLOWING PEOPLE FOR MAKING WTF1 HAPPEN IN 2022...

Aiden Vincent

Alice Powell

AMP

Benjamin Lewis

Bright Partnerships

Cambridge Kisby

Charles Graham

Charles Leclerc

Charles Sargeant

Charley Williams

Chris Gowland

Darren Cox

Daytona Motorsport

DHL

EA Sports

Formula 1

F1 Manager

F1 22

Hannah Prydderch

Harry Eagleton

Jack Benyon

Jamie Chadwick

Jenson Button

Jonathan Reynolds

Jordan Edwards

Josh Suttill

Kyma Media

Matthew Witham

Matt Beer

Naomi Panter

Paul Hanaphy

Paul Ryan

Rory McKie

Sebastian Vettel

Sergio Alvarez

Silverstone

Sophie Rogers

Valentin Khorounzhiy

And, of course...

ALL OF OUR AWESOME TEAM WTF1 MEMBERS

WHERE YOU CAN FIND WTF1

| WTF1.COM | #WTF1 |

FOLLOW US ON SOCIAL

@WTF1OFFICIAL

| TIKTOK | TWITTER |
| INSTAGRAM | FACEBOOK |

LISTEN TO OUR PODCAST

**SEARCH 'WTF1 PODCAST'
IN ALL PODCAST APPS**

WATCH VIDEO + LIVE STREAMS

| TWITCH.COM/WTF1OFFICIAL | YOUTUBE.COM/WTF1OFFICIAL |

OTHER WAYS TO GET INVOLVED

JOIN TEAM WTF1	WTF1.COM/TEAMWTF1
F1 CAMPING @ WTF1 CLUBHOUSE	WTF1.COM/CLUBHOUSE
BUY MERCH @ WTF1 SHOP	SHOP.WTF1.COM

\wtf1.